We're All In This Together

By

Jess Miller

First published in October 2000 by: Jester Publishers, Suite 72, Private Bag X 4, Gordons Bay 7150, South Africa.

Cover Design: Nouveau Design/Jess Miller.
Artwork: Bennie Krüger, Cape Town.

Other titles by Jess Miller: **The Great Convergence** – an uplifting, humorous novel.

Jess Miller's books are distributed privately in the US, UK and South Africa – providing fast and reliable service – full details are available from Jess's self-help Stress & Depression website:

http://www.lifetravellers.com

To arrange for Jess to talk to your group, wherever in the world you might be, or for help with Stress & Depression please email him on:

lifetravellers@lifetravellers.com

Printed and bound in South Africa
Helping to keep previously disadvantaged people in jobs

CONTENTS

Acknowledgements
Introduction

ACKNOWLEDGEMENTS

My thanks go to those who stood by me and helped when I was slipping so quickly from this life, some of whom I list below in the belief that those who do good upon the Earth should forever have their names shouted on high.

Patrick & Wanda Madden, Dr.Carel Bredell, Dr.Frieda Badenhorst, Sister Esther Jones, Andrew Swart, Wendy van Breda, Elzanne van Wyk, Brian Snellgrove, Karen Weisensee, Rita Jones, Hermann Johl, John & Sonia Dippenaar, Helga Bergh, Wiehan van Dyk, John & Lavender Buckland, Jennifer Miller, Peter & Penny Neep and so many more.......

Also to those who are no longer living, but who are still ever present in my life and upon whose strength and wisdom I drew at the most critical of times:

Bernard Miller, Jack Morris, Jimmy MacLean, Jim Duncan.......

Finally to the whole of Nature, the great mountains, rivers, forests, lonely beaches, powerful seas, cold winds, lashing rains and burning suns that have taught me so much about myself and that have nurtured me within their energy.

4

I wrote this book for You.

INTRODUCTION

I am not a doctor, nor a qualified therapist. I am simply someone who feels that the knowledge I have built up throughout my lifetime could be of significant use to You.

Manic depression, anxiety or panic attacks, bi-polar disorders and clinical depression all have similar kinds of effects upon the sufferer, behind those that we see on the surface.

It is these effects, where they come from, what they do to you and what to do about them that many sufferers and people in general do not understand.

By giving up your time and money to purchase this book you have placed upon me your expectation of learning something helpful, meaningful and positive. I promise that I will not let you down.

Awareness will be our key.

Awareness about Stress, Tension, Loneliness and Depression, which I call –

'STLD'

Like most of us I have been through some wonderful and some terrible experiences in my life. One of those that qualified to be placed amongst the terrible was clinical depression, from which it took me some eighteen months to recover to an acceptable state of being.

I am one of the lucky ones.

Some people do not believe that Depression exists.

Some people think Depression might exist, but cannot understand what it is.

Some people live within the grip of Depression everyday.

Those who believe that Depression does not exist and that it is simply used as an excuse to get off work or off life cannot conceive that for some it is the all-consuming condition that is their very existence.

Such people do not recognise that they or someone close to them could be slipping unwittingly further and further into the creeping, insidious darkness of STLD and so they fail to take crucial early steps to stop this deadly slide.

But if more of us become aware, then together we can bring about the quantum change in understanding that is so necessary for preventative measures against the march of STLD to take their proper place in our world.

By all of us becoming fully aware of STLD we will be better prepared to offer our understanding and compassion to its victims and extend a helping hand to those who are suffering from its stranglehold.

Your awareness of the effects and ravages of STLD and how it can affect you and those around you is a paramount understanding critical to our building a world based on the strong foundation of the Power of Love – and I do mean Power, the one and only true Power that we have each been given.

To get the most from this book you will need to apply the greatest amount of self-honesty that you are capable of. If you are not prepared to be one hundred percent honest with yourself then it is possible that you will never win out over STLD.

Take my word for it.

Unless you cast off everything The System of Life has indoctrinated into you and become totally and absolutely honest with yourself, STLD will remain in your life, sapping you of your Energy and your Life Force, debilitating you and keeping you locked in its downward spiral into the Darkness.

You will need even more self-honesty and open mindedness if you are someone who does not believe that STLD exists. Without applying such totally open self-honesty whilst you read this book you will never be truly aware of the awful reality that could be affecting a family member, a loved one or a friend and how you could have helped them through what otherwise might turn into a life threatening experience.

Do you care about your partner?

Your children?

Their children?

Your best friend?

Yourself?

If your answer for some reason is 'No' then read no further, for this book will surely be wasted on you. But if your answer is 'Yes' then be determined to be honest with yourself in order to gain the awareness, the knowledge and the power that will let you win out in the ongoing struggle against STLD.

As we set out together on our journey of learning about the causes of this dreadful condition, what it is like to be in the Darkness and how we can get back to the Light, let us bear in mind at all times how extremely important it is for us to increase our individual level of knowledge concerning:

Stress, Tension, Loneliness and Depression.

CHAPTER 1.

ME.

Some people think that I'm a little strange and I cannot blame them for thinking so.

This is because I have never been truly conventional, although I have dallied (and still do) with convention from time to time. I have always lived the experience of an adventurous life to the fullest. I do not have a religion, nor does a religion have me in the way that I wear its label, and it has been that way since I was some twenty-one years old.

But I believe in God with every fibre of my being and have always done so.

Now before you go saying to yourself 'Oh, here we go, this is going to be all about how I must turn to God or how religion will somehow miraculously save me', I want to tell you that God does indeed form a part of this book, but not in any way other than in which he forms a part of life. We both recognise that how big a part he plays in your life is entirely up to you and I give you my assurance that I will not be asking you to join any religion, go to any religious place of worship, abandon your life's tenets and take up those of some church or dedicate your life to some religious belief.

I will also not be asking you to 'follow me' because I am some sort of guru and 'know the way' (and by the way, give me all your money), or to commit yourself to any of the spiritually religious stuff that I am sure you know only too well. Let us leave all of this aside and not even think about it whilst we travel onward and let me simply tell you my belief about God, because it is of the utmost relevance to our understanding of STLD.

I believe that something, some Being, Force, Power or Spirit, created absolutely everything and to describe that Being, Force, Power or Spirit – I use the word 'God'.

Let's just think about things for a minute.

I am saying that God created the book you are holding, the pages, the type and the cover. He created the clothes you are wearing the house you live in, the car you drive, the street outside, the villages, the towns and the cities. He created the trees, the woods, the forests, the hills, the mountains, the valleys, the rivers, the lakes and the oceans. He created the animals, the fish, the birds, the sky, the heavens, the stars, the universe, the galaxies, the galaxies beyond the galaxies and the galaxies beyond that which our minds can comprehend.

His most incredible Creation.

I am someone who believes that God created all of this and that his hand is upon everything, including you and me.

But I get even stranger.

Now that you understand my belief that God created everything you might also understand why I believe that it was God who created you and me. And if God created us he must have done so with some specific purpose in mind, for surely he would not have gone to all the trouble of creating us just on a whim. The more I have thought about this as I have journeyed through my life, the more I have come to an interesting conclusion.

I believe that God created every human being as a Sacred Spirit upon the Earth.

And this includes You.

I bet you never thought of yourself as a Sacred Spirit, now did you? Having a quiet chuckle? Well to me that is what you are and so is every other human being, whether they are good or evil.

We are Sacred Spirits all.

Another way I think of us, and a description that I am really comfortable with, is that we are all 'Children of God'.

So, to me, not only are you a Sacred Spirit, you are also:

A Child of God.

Now don't start getting bigheaded about this, will you?

As my own life unfolded and took me upon its extraordinary course a feeling grew inside me that I was in reality becoming some kind of LifeTraveller. This simply means I am someone who travels the ups and downs and ins and outs of life, meeting and dealing with the good and the bad experiences, being 'guided' more and more and following what I perceive to be the path God intended for me.

I must impress upon you that I do not consider this 'title' of LifeTraveller as something grand; I just think it describes me pretty well. But then, the more people I have met during my existence and the more stories I have listened to about their fantastic or terrible experiences and, indeed, the more of these kinds of experiences I have shared with them, the more I have come to believe that in reality we are all LifeTravellers, travelling this Road of Life together.

We are all LifeTravellers.

My life has been brimming over with adventure, struggle, triumph and disaster, throughout which there has been one thing that I have perceived to be at work continuously in our world, over and over again in situation after situation, something that I now recognise more than at any previous time:

We're All In This Together.

There are many things that we can each do successfully on our own, but there are many more that we can do even more successfully together and if we want to change ourselves and our world for the better then we must realise that we can only bring about that change if we do it in harmony - together.

After all we care for each other in the world of medicine and healing, we teach each other, we help each other in times of crisis and need, we interact with each other in the making of our livelihoods, our business and our every day life.

So every day, in every way:

We're All In This Together.

And one day my personal declaration, which I would like to share with you now, came to me out of nowhere.

It is a declaration that I suddenly started saying when in the depths of Depression and heading out of this world.

A declaration that I began saying out loud in a simple, open, and honest way to myself and to God, over and over and over again.

It became my standard, my flagship, and my rock of self-declaration, helping me enormously through those dark, forbidding days.

Gradually it's meaning began to change and grow ever stronger, whilst I slowly became able to heal and grow stronger as I made my way back to the Light:

Our Declaration:

I am a Sacred Spirit

I am a Child of God

I am a LifeTraveller

And

We're All In This Together

Whenever you are in trouble - spiritual, physical, stressful or depressive trouble and everything has become too much for you, then say these words both to yourself and to God and turn them into your openly honest declaration of who and what you are.

I promise you that the more you emphasise them and give them a meaning that you alone can create, the more things will begin to happen and change in your life and the more you will begin to understand and accept your own situation as well as the situations of those around you.

This is a declaration that will constantly bring you some perspective amongst the grinding turmoil of our turbulent world.

So if we are Sacred Spirits (please take my word for it just for now!) what is it that we are supposed to be doing here upon the Earth?

Did God intend for us to come here and live a life of drudgery, hatred, jealousy, fear, or a life strangled by any number of other nasty things?

Why would he do something so wasteful?

What might be the real purpose of our being here?

Just to annoy everyone else?

Or to grab as much as we can for ourselves and then learn only at the end that which we ignored all along, that we simply cannot take it with us?

Did he create us only to seek power over others and then defend that power by having to exercise control over all other Sacred Spirits?

Or did he intend for us to live a life of loving, helping, caring, understanding, learning, teaching, and healing?

I began thinking about the answer to these questions a long, long time ago, but every time I did so something would keep getting in the way, stopping my ability to think about them long enough and deeply enough to be able to reach a satisfactory conclusion.

Surely, I reasoned, God could not have intended for us to be born to carry out any of these lesser ways of living and for us just to accept them as being the right way that we should live our lives?

Surely there must be a better way, a way where Sacred Spirits can cease living their lives hating, fearing and hurting each other?

But whenever my thoughts lingered along these lines something kept on sidetracking me, filling my life with a host of problems that consumed my energy and distracting me from reaching the answer. It was a long, long time before I fully understood what it was that kept blocking me.

It was The System of Life.

CHAPTER 2.

THE SYSTEM OF LIFE.

The System both constricts and contains us all our lives within its all-pervading power.

It teaches us how and what to think, it educates us throughout our critical formative years, it places us on the merry-go-round of having to earn a living in order to exist and it ensures that through both direct and indirect taxation and from governmental fiscal profligacy to world food supply the bulk of Sacred Spirits are entrapped and enmeshed within its spidery web.

The more you become immersed within its power, the less time you have for You. That is why for such a long time, because of my lifetime of indoctrination by The System, the answer to my questioning the way we live had eluded me.

Then, through my experience of STLD, I began to realise that I had known the answer, as well as the answer to the question of why we are here, all along. But because of the System's blocking force I had never quite been able to clearly recognise or understand these answers. And so I came to make the retrospective discovery that, for me, there are two real reasons, above all others as to why we are here.

We are here to learn.

We are here to do good upon the Earth.

As a child I learned from my elders, who had themselves learned great wisdom in their lifetimes, and they taught me all kinds of wondrous things, constantly opening up my mind and my world to new learning experiences. The older they were the more wisdom they seemed to have and the kindlier they seemed and the more constructively instructive. And then, just as I had begun to feed upon and get to grips with the fantastic knowledge they were imparting to me, they were gone, simply taken away, leaving me at a complete standstill in the lonely void of their leaving.

'For heaven's sake what can possibly be the point of gaining all this wonderful knowledge throughout your life and then, when you rise to the level of actually being a real live sage who can impart this knowledge to others, saving them years of time spent in learning it for themselves, you die?' I asked myself.

I simply could not understand it.

The type of knowledge which my elders had been imparting to me when I was younger we might call 'physical' knowledge. Knowledge of the sort of things that

I would be able to understand at a young age. But I have come to realise that it is an all-encompassing journey of knowledge that we are on and that knowledge of things alone is not enough.

Much more is required of us.

It is necessary for us to gain real knowledge of ourselves, our spirituality and the meaning and purpose of our lives within God's Great Scheme. Our spirituality belongs to each of us individually; it is like a contract with our Creator. It is not the preserve of religions or gurus.

Your spirituality belongs to you and to no one else. It is the relationship between you and God to do with as you will. You can choose to ignore it or you can learn about it, develop it and live by how you feel it assists you in your life.

We also need to develop knowledge about God, his constant presence and his willingness to help us if only we could push The System of Life to the side and open our eyes and our hearts to him. He has placed us here to learn so many things that sometimes we may need his help in order to do so.

We are here to learn how to coexist, how to expand our virtues, how to work out the best values to live our lives by, how we are capable of good and evil and which of those two roads we are going to decide to take and, most importantly of all in our journey of learning:

We are here to learn how to be.

I then 'discovered' another retrospective insight. You cannot learn these things without being absolutely, completely and totally honest with yourself at all times. However, our indoctrination by The System has made this an extremely difficult task for the mass of Sacred Spirits to undertake. They hide in their life's training of lying to each other or to themselves (and therefore living a lie), or in fear based lives resulting in their inability to operate from the foundation of true self-honesty and so they remain firmly entrenched within the clutches of The System.

You've heard a lot of this before, I'm sure, and you've most probably dismissed much of it as rubbish, as I did earlier on in my life. But because I have now had a thorough firsthand examination of the way The System works on us, thrust upon me via STLD, I can see how it may have so easily led to your having dismissed thinking about these kinds of things.

Many of us live our lives locked on autopilot. We 'enjoy' the 'safety' of our repetitive daily life and our time is consumed so much by everything we either have to or try to do, that we are never allowed time to think about ourselves in any spiritual way. We just keep on keeping on, for better or for worse.

Living our world in this way gets us lost in the tussle of everyday life, lost within the time consuming barrage that the System throws at us. Lost in life.

O.K., so what do you do when you get lost on a car journey? You either turn around and go back to a point that you recognise or you stop and ask someone the way. If the first person you ask cannot help you then you keep asking until you find someone who can. Right?

If we begin to realise that we have had our lives locked up by The System then we need to seek out and ask one of the Sacred Spirits who have been able to think deeply about themselves and have managed to come to the understanding that there is very much more to life than just living on autopilot under the influence of The System. That there is so much more to be done with our lives than just to quietly give in to that influence.

So I ask that you please humour me and accept that there is a possibility that God is alive and well and is here to help each of us with our journey, if only we would access him.

Accept that there is also the possibility that we are here to undertake an immense learning experience, no matter how terrible or benign an experience that may be.

Accept that there is also a possibility there may be a different purpose for each of our lives than the one which The System has been kidding us there is, and which consequently may so far have eluded us.

Now that we have reached a point where you are probably wondering why the heck you bought this book in the first place, let us turn and travel together in a different direction.

CHAPTER 3.

YOU.

What are You?

What exactly are You?

I don't mean whether you are a man or a woman, or animal, vegetable or mineral for that matter.

I mean what exactly are You?

A person, of course, but when I talk to you, as I am doing through the words of this book, who or what is it that I am talking to? Am I talking to your big toe? Your foot? Your knee? Your chest? Your chin? Your ear? Your hair?

I don't think so. We do not talk to each other's bodies. So what is the thing that is reading these words, assimilating and digesting the information, reacting to it and deciding what to do with it?

Surely that is the real You, isn't it?

So I ask you again. What are You?

See if you can answer this question for yourself before you read on.

You are, are you not (and please correct me with a bold red pen if I am wrong) a Living Consciousness that is occupying your body for this gigantic learning experience that we are all on?

You are not your body.

You are a wonderful living consciousness that is occupying your body whilst you are undergoing this learning experience, and it is **that** You to whom I am talking, the very Living Consciousness that is the real You.

O.K.?

When God breathed his life into you and you entered this world, I believe that you were born as a totally pure Spirit. No, I'm not kidding. Oh, perhaps you brought some undesirable qualities with you that would show up later in your life, but right back there at the commencement of your existence upon Earth I believe that you were a truly pure Spirit. Your consciousness was clear and untainted, open and pure in a way that it would never be again, for no sooner were you born than along came The System and clamped its vicelike hold upon you.

The very first things that you learned to do were to cry, eat and poop and, boy, were you good at those! But then you started to learn other things as The System began an indoctrination of You, the Living Consciousness, that would continue for the rest of your life.

You learned about happiness, disappointment, pain, harmony, losing, winning, cheating, lying, fearing, dreading, terror, hate, love, beauty, right, wrong, humour, temptation, wanting, yearning, desiring, learning, money, materialism, relationships, broken hearts, business, responsibility, wealth, poverty, danger, safety and a whole myriad of other things.

It hardly seems possible that, as The System threw this wall of 'life' at you, you had any time at all to really learn about yourself.

Throughout this indoctrination you learned above all how to become the greatest of reactionaries, reacting instantaneously to absolutely everything that came your way. From having other kids steal your toys, to suffering your parents anger or receiving their love, to big scary monsters, teachers, bullies, sounds, sights and feelings, they all taught you to react, but they never taught you to think about your reactions, they just made you react instinctively.

I mean, you most probably never asked yourself why you were scared of something and never trained yourself to control that instant reaction to fear that could paralyse you.

In amongst all this mass of indoctrination there were two classic examples of the way your reactionary behaviour became embedded into your psyche and it is important, in the light of STLD, for us to take a look at these two now.

They are Hate and Fear.

CHAPTER 4.

HATE AND FEAR.

You went to your first school only to find that somebody there hated you. Why? Was it because of your race, colour, physical appearance or your weakness? Pretty soon, in order to survive, you were learning to hate as well. When the bigger boys or girls said that they hated someone you somehow found yourself agreeing that you hated them as well. If you didn't hate who it was that they hated, you received a thumping. You automatically began finding things to hate as a natural defence to mask your own weakness and fears and as a survival technique in your school environment.

Or maybe it was your parents who showed you hate for certain kinds of people? Did you hear them always saying how they hated certain people on television? If you did then this indoctrination of dislike was sinking in and becoming a part of You. The System of Life was indoctrinating you to hate through those who were teaching you, along with the help of peer pressure, and this was the start of how you began to be turned into The Great Reactionary.

Almost everything we do is a reaction to something. Unfortunately we hardly think about the bulk of these reactions – we just react.

How many times have we each reacted swiftly to something or someone, only to instantly regret having done so?

The System bombards us with all kinds of stuff that we have to constantly react to and, within our reactionary workings, our reaction to instantly hate something stands strong.

You understand, don't you, that countless millions of Sacred Spirits live their entire lives upon the Earth completely enveloped in hatred? Some hate races, some hate people's colours, some hate religions, some hate those of different political persuasions, some hate those with wealth, etc.

They spend their lives indoctrinating those around them to hate who or what it is that they hate and then they use this indoctrination to be able to control the very people they have been indoctrinating.

What an abject waste of the greatest gift of all gifts - their lives.

So let's bring Hate into perspective. Here is a simple little exercise.

Close your eyes and think of the thing that you hate or dislike the most in this world. Make sure you set it up really big in your mind, so that there is nothing else in the picture apart from this thing that you intensely hate or dislike.

Got it?

Then ask yourself this question:

What is hate?

Keep thinking of that thing you hate or dislike and keep asking yourself the question:

What is hate?

Do this exercise now. Do it over and over for as long as it takes until you feel something change within you .... and only then read on.

If you do this exercise long enough and really concentrate on your hate and question yourself about what that hate really is, you might find yourself feeling just a tad silly after a while. I mean, after all, what is hate? It can be a hard emotion to understand. Why do you hate? Where did your hate come from? How come you have such little control over it?

Hate is the weakness of convenience. On the outside it appears to be strength, but this mirage is nothing but the false façade of weakness. It is often seemingly more excusable, convenient and accepted by others for us to show hate than love. But hate is not natural. It is not something that you have to do. It is not a given thing, it is not forced upon you, it is not inherent in your make up and it is most certainly not a condition of your being here. Hate is generated and created by only one source and one source alone and that source, my friend, is You.

You create hate out of feelings of fear and inadequacy, a longing for acceptance by others, as a defence or as the fear driven, weak domination of the bully. It was not there before you created it and you alone are the creator and operator of your hate. It is not something that has a mind control ability of its own, until you give it one.

FEAR

Fear is the blood brother of hate. Fear is the major means of controlling and manipulating the masses of Sacred Spirits upon our planet. Fear of everything from lack of money, to lack of power, to the breakdown of a relationship, to failing in life, to death. Fear is an underlying false basis to so much of our behaviour.

Let me give you a great example of what I mean.

I met a lady who was just the nicest person and she and her husband very kindly gave me dinner. We chatted about everything you can possibly imagine. It was 1999 in South Africa. After dinner she suddenly said to me,

"I'm absolutely terrified that we are going to have a civil war. I think about it all the time and cannot get it out of my mind."

I talked with her for a little while, just feeling my way after this astonishing statement, and then she said,

"I have this dreadful feeling that hordes of people are coming to rape, torture and murder me in the foulest of ways."

'Hold on a bit' I thought to myself as I looked around to see if hordes of attackers were coming swarming over the hill. Then later she said,

"I'm so frightened that I'm going to be afflicted with a terrible disease that is going to give me such pain for the rest of my life."

'Ah-ha,' thought I, 'this is not going to be so easy, Jess, old bean.'

But she wasn't finished, for it then transpired that she was even more terrified of dying.

I took a deep breath and began to ask her questions.

"Do we have a civil war?"

"No. But we might."

"But we might not."

"But we might."

"But if we did, wouldn't you do something to protect yourself and your family? Wouldn't you make sure you moved to a safe area or left the country? You would have time you know, civil wars don't start at the touch of a button, they build slowly from sporadic incidents that harden attitudes on both sides, so you would have plenty of warning."

She thought about this. Then I asked her,

"And where are these hordes of people who are coming to kill you? Are they on their way?"

"Oh, no. I just feel that they might be coming to kill me."

"But they might not."

"But they might."

"And if hordes of people were on the move, coming specifically to kill you, don't you think we'd hear about it? Don't you think we'd all rally round, get you to take evasive action, protect you and move you to safety?"

"Well, yes, I suppose so, but I have this dreadful feeling that one day they are going to come."

"But they're not coming right now?"

"No."

"They're not even on their way, are they?"

"No."

"Phew! That's a great relief. And who said you are going to be afflicted with this terrible illness that will make you live in dreadful pain for the rest of your life?"

"No one, I'm just terrified about it."

"But are you in good health?"

"Yes."

"So is there any reason to suspect that you are going to get such an affliction?"

"No. Not really. I'm just terrified that I might."

"But you might not."

"But I might."

"And if somehow you did, although the odds are against it, don't you think the doctors would do everything for you that they could to limit your pain? They would even give you Morphine and Cocaine to knock you out if it was necessary. But I see no reason to suppose that this is going to happen to you, you'll probably live to a ripe old age and be a considerable nuisance to your grandchildren." She laughed.

"And why are you frightened about death?"

"Oh, I'm sure I'm going to die in a really bad way, something painful and horrible."

"But you might just go to bed one night and not wake up the next day."

"Well, I might."

"Sure. In fact my best friend's mother sat down before Sunday lunch with her favourite newspaper in one hand and a gin and tonic in the other and simply left us. So I have reason to believe that the odds are good that you may not even know about it. Anyway isn't dying as natural as being born?"

That threw her a bit and I knew I had overstepped the mark, but we chatted on for some time and then she said to me,

"I'm being a bit silly about all this, aren't I?"

"Not in the slightest, you are only doing what the System has taught you to do all your life, build up fear about certain things that don't exist and then have them drain you of your Energy. You'll probably get Cancer if you go on worrying like this, you know. I have to tell you that just as easily as you created all these things that you are terrified of, none of which exist, you can let them go. All you have to do is to let them go and get on and enjoy your life."

Some time later I saw her and her husband again and what a change. A much stronger Sacred Spirit appeared, with purpose in her life and she told me she needed another good boost to keep her going, so there I was, talking away to her for more hours, trying to help her keep on the wonderful road of strength she had discovered.

What is really devastating about all of this is that this lady had set up four imaginary Fear Centres – Civil War, Torture/Murder, Affliction and Death.

Now if you are someone who does this you become the Master or Mistress of Creativity whilst you create such Fear Centres and then, blow me sideways, you go and give them all your Energy.

It's quite incredible. You create these things out of nothing and then you give them all your Life Force, which results in you immediately losing control of your life to your very own false creations, whilst all the time there they sit, rubbing their hands in glee, saying 'Give me more of your Energy, give me more!' and so, miserably, you oblige the wishes of what are nothing more in reality than abject, non-existent impostors.

Just think about the hundreds of millions of Sacred Spirits who either hate or fear each other, having created these two massive Power Draining Centres out of nothing and there they are, living out their existence stuck in a life of giving all their Life Force and Energy to fictitious creations of entirely their own making.

Now you know why I say 'What a waste'.

Employing the same exercise that we used for Hate can really help you let go of your Fears.

Just take one of your Fears at a time, make them the biggest picture in your mind and keep asking yourself this question:

What is Fear?

CHAPTER 5.

LOVE.

"Oh, don't talk to me about all that mushy silliness. I think that people who talk about Love and God are weak!"

So said someone to me not so long ago. This was a power person, wrapped up in their daily fight to gain riches, crushing the opposition and crushing those in their employ if they either stepped out of line or didn't produce the goods.

Love has nothing to do with all that kissy-kissy 'I love you' stuff that people flaunt so easily at each other, as if it somehow excuses and absolves them of actions that might be somewhat less than loving. It has nothing to do with any 'mushy silliness' and it most certainly has nothing whatsoever to do with weakness.

Love is quite simply the most powerful force on the planet – bar none – and what is more it has been given to each of us individually. In fact Love is the absolute and purest Power that we have within us, a force that can heal, help, bring together, solve problems, save and forgive. All the other things that we perceive as being power are not really power at all. They are things that man has created. There is so called 'power' over power-pyramids everywhere you look. Military power? Man's creation. The President of the United States? The head of another so called 'power' pyramid. The more I think about everything that we call 'power' I can find only one that is true, one that was put inside all of us by God and not created by man.

So what in actual fact is Love? As I have said it is the most powerful force on the planet – bar none. But where does it come from and how can it be so powerful? It doesn't appear magically of its own accord. It won't appear at all if you sit on your hands and whistle for it. Love comes from deep within you, from your own desire to operate by its power to make your life and the lives of those around you better and, by doing so, your world as a whole a better place. So how do you do this? How can you begin to operate from the Power of Love and how can you use it to win out over all those other weak emotions we have just examined, the ones that are cluttering up your life and draining you of your Energy?

What has happened is that the System has bludgeoned out of us our ability and our will to connect with the Power of Love that we have each been given and it has managed to sever us from our ability to be who and what we really are. I say that because I believe that on the day that God breathed his life into every Sacred Spirit upon this earth, (that includes you, remember?), he made each of us as a 100% Loving Being.

The opposite of Hate is Love.

Hate is Weakness - Love is Strength.

The System tries its utmost to get us to believe the very opposite and it makes a very convincing case to con us with, but the proof is there for each of us to find out for ourselves if we want to. We misguidedly think that Love is somehow weak, that the only way we are supposed to exist is to be rough and tough and carve out for ourselves that which we want in life and fight tooth and nail against everyone else and beat them down to get it.

Boy, do we miss the point big time.

If we Sacred Spirits were all to operate from the Power of Love then nothing, absolutely nothing could stop our contribution to this world from making the biggest and most positive difference to everything that is wrong with humanity.

This means that you <u>can</u> make a difference.

Just imagine a world where all six billion Sacred Spirits spent their time doing good for each other by operating from the Power of Love.

42

Hard to imagine, isn't it?

In a short while I will show you how all of us can operate from the Power of Love

CHAPTER 6.

MAKING A DIFFERENCE.

Do you think that you don't matter?

Do you think that your life is of no consequence?

Do you think that you cannot make any difference in this world?

Do you think that your life is insignificant within the Great Scheme of things?

Well, let's see, shall we?

I want you to go around for the next twenty-four hours with a great big permanent smile on your face and see what happens. You know what the reaction will be, don't you? Everyone is going to smile right back at you. You put out a smile and you get a smile back. But how can this be when you are so totally insignificant and cannot make a difference? How can you possibly have such an effect upon other people? Because you are not insignificant, just as the life of every Sacred Spirit upon this Earth is not insignificant. That is why.

You attract and receive back what you put out. If you put out moaning, dismal, loser type vibrations in your life then those are the people that you will attract and that is what you will receive back. If you put out greed then greed is what you will attract. If you live your life in hatred then hatred is what you put out and get back and hatred is what will rub off on every single person you come into contact with and it is hatred that will permeate throughout your society. If you live your life wearing a smile then that is what you put out and that is what you get back and that is what will rub off on everyone around you and permeate in exactly the same way.

So if you were to live your life from an all consuming basis of Love for yourself (which is self respect for the way you live your life), for your fellow Sacred Spirits and for this incredible planet that we have been given to live out our existence upon, then Love is what will rub off on everyone you come into contact with and Love is what will permeate throughout your society. Difficult to believe?

You could easily prove it to yourself. Here is an example:

I once had a neighbour in Scotland who I was at loggerheads with. He was a farmer and his land bordered mine. His lawyers besieged me day and night with the most ridiculous problems and he went around the locale spreading false, malicious rumours about me.

He hated me, although he didn't really know me.

Truth was he hated everyone.

One evening I was standing looking out over the trout loch by my cottage. Big Rainbow trout were slurping their evening meal from the surface. The sun was going down in the West (fortunately) and a Highland Piper began playing his bagpipes away up on the hill and the skirl of the pipes came drifting down the glen to me.
It was a beautiful and special evening.

There and then I decided that all of these problems had to stop, so I marched straight up to the farmhouse and knocked on the door. His wife took fright when she saw the enemy standing on her doorstep and he certainly took his time coming from within the depths of the house. When he did his eyes told a story of evil intent and he brusquely asked me what I wanted.

"I've come to tell you that all these problems between us are not of my making and that I would like them to stop and I also came to tell you that I am not your enemy and that I love you and respect you as a fellow human being."

Immediately I had said it I turned and walked. I didn't wait for his reply. I didn't even know why I had said it, I just turned and walked and, as I did so, I felt something very strange, something I had not felt before.

Everything had changed.

The further I walked the better I felt and when I got home I felt as though all my problems had been resolved, which I knew they hadn't, but it certainly felt like they had.

Two days later the farmer came to me and mumbled something about wanting to get on better too and then he started haranguing me about all the things his lawyers had been going on about, in the middle of which I gave him the unexpected present of two trout that I had caught that morning and told him they were for him and his wife and that I hoped they enjoyed them.

At this he was completely flummoxed.

A week later he arrived at my door with a pannier of beautiful fresh vegetables and mumbled that he and his wife had been in their kitchen garden and would I like them? I said that indeed I would and how grateful I was and would he like to come in and have a cup of tea, seeing that I was about to have one? I convinced him to do so with some difficulty and, as we drank our tea, I told him that we were lucky people to be able to live in such a beautiful place.

One year he actually wished me a Merry Christmas, which was nothing short of a miracle.

So what had happened?

I did not fully understand it until many years later. I had almost unwittingly, out of my desperation to change things, gone from being reactive to proactive within the situation. But what had that feeling been that had grown in me as I walked away from him that first time?

Strength.

It had been the strength that emanates from the Power of Love. I had unwittingly made a totally loving act towards a fellow Sacred Spirit, whom I disliked and who hated me, and that very act of Love in all its powerful, wonderful glory would be the catalyst that would change our relationship for the better. I had put out Love and I had received Love back. Not hate. I could have gone and punched his lights out in hatred, all that would have done would have been to make the situation much, much worse and there I would have been, with the weak falsehood of my hatred eagerly consuming my Life Force. But because I acted from some deep well of Love hidden within me, its sheer power saved us both. He had been overwhelmed to receive it and I had been surprised at myself for giving it.

But how it had worked.

The Power of Love is a truly amazing thing to behold and it is something that God specifically placed within you and that you alone have the ability to turn on (and leave turned on permanently) and utilise to the benefit of yourself and all those you come into contact with.

Let me give you another example of the Power of Love:

During the 1970's and early 1980's I had a huge black Labrador called Jake.

Alias: Big Jake, Shaky Jake and Jake the Rake.

One day in the early 70's Jake and I had to get to Kirkwall in the Orkney Islands, to the North East of Scotland in a hurry, but the ferry operators were on strike. I happened to find a small private aircraft company at Edinburgh airport who were willing to hire me a twin engine aircraft for a ridiculously small amount of money, because they had no bookings.

It was blowing a gale when we turned up at the airport all ready to go, only to find that the pilot went into a flat panic when he saw Jake. He refused point blank to take the dog in the aircraft. No way was he going in an aircraft with a dog again as he had already had a serious problem once before.

Jake, although a big, strong, powerful looking dog had the gentlest of natures, got on with everybody and was never any trouble. He had been in aircraft before, on fishing boats and in fast cars and took it all in his stride. In fact on one particularly nasty day, when we had been out in the English Channel, he had raced around the heaving deck all day having a whale of a time, whilst I had hung on for dear life as the seas broke over us.

I had no option but to try and convince the pilot to take us. It took me fully half an hour of explaining to him about

Jake and how there would not be a problem. It was a difficult situation as every dog owner would swear there would not be a problem with their dog, but if they were wrong you could be up there with a serious problem that had teeth at one end of it. I sympathised with the pilot, but I knew that Shaky Jake was only liable to lick him to death, if anything.

After using all my powers of persuasion the pilot hesitatingly agreed and we finally walked out to the aircraft.

"Get up there." I said to Jake and he jumped up on the wing.

"Go on in there," and he jumped into the four-seat cabin and sat in the front.

"Go on in the back." I instructed, and he jumped over into the back and sat there wagging his tail and looking at the astonished pilot. The pilot shot me a glance of disbelief at what he had seen and we got into the plane.

He warned me that it would be rough up to 3000 feet but smooth thereafter and we took off into the teeth of the gale. Rough it was, but Jake just sat there totally unconcerned and looked out of the window. I remember wondering what must have been going through his mind, but although we usually communicated telepathically I found that at that moment I simply could not tell his thoughts.

The flight progressed and became smooth, as the pilot had predicted. After a while he took his headphones off, which he was wearing over his peaked cap, and turned to me to speak, whereupon something suddenly removed his hat smartly from his head and he gave a startled jump.

I smiled and told him to look behind. There sat Big Jake with the peaked cap in his mouth, beating his tail against the side of the aircraft in glee. He gave me the hat back and I gave it back to the ruffled pilot, telling him that Jake liked to carry people's hats and not to worry about it.

He put the hat back on and then turned to tell me what he had originally been going to say, whereupon Jake promptly grabbed his hat again.

We flew into Kirkwall and landed and my friends were there to meet us. There was just one problem. I could not get Jake away from the pilot, who was petting him and playing with him and letting him carry his hat.

Telepathically I communicated to Jake that we should go, but his response was,
'Not yet, look, I've got this guy eating out of the palm of my paw. Just look at him, he loves me. This is the same guy that was terrified of me back in Edinburgh and now look at him. I've cured him! Me! Not You! Me! I've cured him of his fear of dogs. I am so brilliant! Aren't I?'

Well I couldn't really argue with that, so we stood and tried to talk with the pilot, who was not in the least bit interested in us, only in Jake. Eventually, however, I managed to part them with a stern word to the dog, who told me not to be so pathetic, and off we went.

The Power of Love, administered by a huge black Labrador to a fearful human, had expelled all the fear, doubt and worry and had helped that human being at a deep level. You may not think it was Love, that it was just a dog playing, but if you had seen the two of them on the ground in Kirkwall and the complete change in the pilot, you would have to have agreed that the bond of friendship that had grown so quickly between them was indeed borne out of the strength of Love.

So what has all this got to do with Stress, Tension, Loneliness and Depression? Well, we're about to come to that, but first it was necessary for us both to understand a few crucial things and get them straight in our minds.

The points I have been making are that you are a Living Consciousness and that you are, or that you can be, a wholly Loving Being in full control of weak emotions that can inflict such damage upon you, that God has a part to play in your life and that you do indeed have a valuable part to play in the Great Scheme. But for all of this to happen you have to push the clutches of The System aside and stand before God in complete and open honesty.

Open honesty with yourself and himself at all times.

I am a Sacred Spirit

I am a Child of God

I am a LifeTraveller

And

We're All In This Together

CHAPTER 7.

STRESS.

Just as we each have different metabolisms so do we each have a different resistance threshold to Stress. Some can go and fight a war and dismiss it as a tea party, whilst for others a tea party is a stressful event. For some (and I used to be this way) a physical challenge or physical hardship is a playground, for others it is a nightmare. Noisy birds calling or neighbour's dogs barking can lead some of us to distraction, whilst others can sleep quite happily under the flight path of a major airport.

So we all have a different threshold of being able to withstand Stress and it is our lack of awareness and understanding about this fact that keeps us from being able to recognise how and when Stress is affecting either ourselves or someone we know.

Stress is a degree of worry, fear, fretting, concern, pressure, failure, shock, trauma, disaster, loneliness, unhappiness or a feeling of being 'lost' in life.

Stress is the first step, the first warning, the first red danger signal on the road to Depression.

When The System gets hold of you and begins your indoctrination in 'Life' it unleashes a rampant deluge of forces upon your senses that never stops. It pounds you day in and day out with the Noise of Life, which is made up of all the things that your mind has to think about everyday of your existence, such as:

Learning, Planning, Working, Earning, Shopping, Cooking, Encouraging, Looking After, Delegating, Worrying, Fearing, etc.

These and all the others you can think of are the day-to-day things you have to think about and cope with in order to exist, but whilst all this Noise is going on the System also uses the Artillery Bombardment to rain down upon you some of the following problems to give you even more Stress:

War.
Death of a close relative/partner/or friend.
Marriage/Divorce/Separation.
Injury or Illness
Overbearing parents.
Bullying
Retirement
Moving House
Job Loss
Serious ill health within close family
Pregnancy
New Baby
Work Problems
Family Arguments
Financial overheads
Loneliness
New Job

Sexual Problems
Children starting or finishing school
Child leaving home
Change in living conditions
Involvement in legal action
Breaking the law/arrest/prison sentence
Drug Addiction
Alcohol Addiction

And of course many, many more.

So there you are, this wonderful Living Consciousness that has its own specific resistance level to Stress, having to withstand everything that The System can throw at you in a constant bombardment day in and day out.

A lot of the time stressful events and traumas are not always that obvious. Being abused physically or sexually as a child is the deepest kind of trauma that can stay with the victim for a lifetime before surfacing, if it ever does. But even moving home is an extremely stressful undertaking, and yet it is hard for most of us to see it as such. The severing of your roots, your foundations, your feelings for your home, your feelings of comfort and security, all are traumatic. Maybe you are moving to a place where you don't know anyone and you won't even know where to go shopping. This creates a deep, underlying fear in you, which brings us to the biggest stress of all:

The Fear of the Unknown.

The more superficial a fear is, like someone jumping out at you and shouting 'Boo!', the less the extent of its damage, but the deeper down inside you that a fear and its associated stress are able to work, the greater their impact upon your conscious and subconscious.

An example of 'superficial' fear is:

The Big Scary Monster.

When The Big Scary Monster appears your fear does not come from the monster. It doesn't wear a placard saying 'I'm a Big Scary Monster so be frightened of me', it doesn't give fear to you or generate fear within you because it can't – you allow that fear to manifest, to generate – you are the creator of your fear, not the Monster, it just stands there. It may not even be remotely interested in you. It might be tired, have indigestion, be lost or looking for a pub. But there you go and allow incredible fear to manifest within you, because that is the automatic reaction The System has taught you to have whenever you see a Big Scary Monster.

I have a really strange belief about this kind of fear.

If the Big Scary Monster appears what are you going to do?

57

Execute that greatest of all military commands – 'Run away!'?

Or are you going to hide?

Whichever it is you are going to do your best to avoid the Monster, aren't you? But if that Big Scary Monster comes for you and is going to kill you and you have taken every possible avoiding action available to you, to no avail, then something is about to happen that is meant to be. If it is your time it is your time and neither you nor I can alter that fact.

So what on earth is the point of being frightened about it then?

Does your fear of what is about to happen help you to get away? Does it help you hide? Oh, yes, you may argue that it is a perfectly natural reaction, but I would agree that it is only so because that is how The System has taught you to react. Were the Big Scary Monster to catch and kill you all the fear in the world would not have been one iota of help, would it? Your being afraid would not have made one shred of difference. If you think about that fact then why do we allow ourselves to create fears of all kinds of things in our life that are utterly undeserving of such fears?

Fear breaks you down – it never builds you up.

Let us look at an example of the other kind of fear, the Fear of the Unknown, and here is something I have seen happen time and time again.

A man works for 40 years in the same job, retires and dies of a heart attack within a very short space of time. Why does this happen? It is because for 40 years he has had the security of a foundation in his life, a regime that has embedded a comfort level in his very core being. He has no Fear of the Unknown because he knows everything that happens in his life, working as he does to the beat of the same drum day in and day out for all those years. Then he retires and the foundation that he has built his life upon, that solid comfort level that has cocooned him for such a long time, is suddenly gone.

Now he is thrust into the void of the Unknown, where that greatest of all fears lurks. The routine is gone. He has all the time in the world now, but to do what? He knows little other than what he worked at for all those years and even attempting to take up a hobby will be a trauma of a kind as he swims in the void that is his new life.

Deep, deep down he has a fear of this massive change in his life and either consciously or subcon͘sly he will be asking himself if this is what he wor͠ ͠se years to achieve. His solid foundation has a deep, underlying stress that he has before and it is this stress that will brin͘ that will kill him.

This is a measure of how serious the deep, underlying Stress that emanates from the Fear of the Unknown is to any Sacred Spirit.

The fact that we do not recognise this Stress in either others or ourselves is perfectly understandable. But these are the underlying emotions and forces that we have got to think deeply about, because it is they who will be our undoing, either quickly, as in the case of a heart attack, or slowly over many years as in a descent into Depression. Being aware of these things could prove to be of crucial benefit either to you or those around you.

Do you think you can handle or take whatever life throws at you?

Do you know where your Stress Threshold is?

Have you ever even thought about it?

Are you sure?

Maybe your threshold, your inability to cope with the Stresses and Traumas in your life is not as high as you thought it was and that secretly and insidiously these Stresses and Traumas have been surreptitiously forcing you, the Living Consciousness, down the road of Stress, Tension, Loneliness and Depression for a long time.

The more disastrous, traumatic, awful or disappointing things that happen to you and the more you hold them inside, the more your ability to withstand such Stresses is eroded and your resistance threshold is approached. This can happen over a period of years and years – even from dreadful things that happened to you in your childhood – until one day your Stress Threshold is finally breached.

Gradually your consciousness, the real You, becomes beaten down and finds itself not being able to take in and process everything it is hearing and seeing, everything the System is bombarding it with. Gradually, almost imperceptibly, it slips into the clutches of STLD, until one day something dreadful occurs or the build up of Stress finally becomes overwhelming and tips You, the Living Consciousness, over the edge of the precipice.

I wrote some verse that tells the story of this process:

The Slippery Slope

You get a toy and find it breaks
Your Mother hits you - your heart aches

You hate your food and you get ill
And you're so sick, they give you pills
You hate to swallow or to chew
Painful needles stuck in you
For your own good, or so they say
To make your illness go away
From all this pain you try to hide
And then you're told your parents died

You're running on the Slippery Slope

At school it's strange and smells and noise
And punches come from other boys
And all the teachers you don't like
Nor can you understand their tripe
And you get hit upon your head
And you were, Oh, so nearly dead
And now you see all things in double
Leading you to different troubles

You're running on the Slippery Slope

And pressure comes to pass exams
And failure hurts your pride and lands
You in a job you just can't stand
Whilst friends who passed are doing well
And you are nothing in your eyes
But worse is coming, your surprise

The one you love is getting wed
With someone else they'll be in bed
From now on you are on your own
Unloved, uncared for
Home alone

You're running on the Slippery Slope

Or you're a housewife doing chores
Your baby cries, your husband snores
Your child gets sick, you lose your job
Your husband leaves, the lazy slob
You clean and cook and sew and wash
You teach and nurse and shop and dash
Around just every day
And every day's the same old way
No Life, no Love, no Strength, no Friend
You think you're going round the bend

You're running on the Slippery Slope

And all the time off in the wings
Satan's chuckling as these things
All pound your head day in, day out
Now even small things make you jump
And in your breast they've found a lump
Your Fear's so great it even clouds
Your judgement - you get sick

And your child dies and you are kicked
Out into touch
Not in the game any longer
Just in name

You're running on the Slippery Slope

Or you're a Military fighter brave
Taught your feelings to enslave
Sent to war to kill your foe
A mirror of you - that you know
Your training makes you good at killing
And blind obedience makes you willing
But deep inside these feelings rest
And pains begin to burn your chest
And finally after years and years
They rise to choke your life as fears
You never paid attention to
You had them, now they've got you.

You're running on the Slippery Slope

Protect your kids from GM foods
Mad cow disease and awful Flu's
If you want Up, don't watch the News
They're killing people just like you
Around the world, what can you do?
Your world gone mad with the power of Bad

Raping, murdering, torturing, starving
Every day in every way it's in your face
Won't go away
Silently eating you deep inside
Where the worst of Fears all tend to hide

You're running on the Slippery Slope

The hopes, the fears, the toll of years
The lies, deceit, the kick of feet
The punch, the drunk, the friend - the skunk
The businesses you had, now defunct
The money gone, the bills unpaid
The school fees coming round again
The medical bills, the lack of thrills
No helping hand, No Jack and Jill
The System's got you in its grasp
And it won't let go 'til your last gasp

You're running on the Slippery Slope

Friends all leave you, lovers deceive you
Rules are broken, lies are spoken
Hopes are gone, you stagger on
Doctors try to help their best
Pills and medicines you ingest
But Loneliness still dogs your heels
And no one knows just how you feel

Empty, desolate, frightened, desperate
A rudderless vessel on a stormy sea
A shadow of who you used to be

You're running on the Slippery Slope

You run and run against the flow
But down the Slippery Slope you go
Running, running, running slow
Your progress charted backwards now
The running sweat upon your brow
You never felt this downward trend
That hurtled you towards the end
Of what you knew as life before
And you become just one more
Broken Sacred Spirit
Who finds that they can run no more
So finally you are on the floor of life

The slope has ended, you're in free fall
Into the Darkness that beats them all

The Darkness of Depression

Jess Miller. 2000.

I am a Sacred Spirit

I am a Child of God

I am a LifeTraveller

And

We're All In This Together

Chapter 8.

THE DARKNESS.

And in the Darkness you cannot see.

It is a place of enormous pain and heartache, of the greatest Fear and Loneliness. It is a surreal place where your mind flits from one thought to another, racing on and on in a kind of desperation. You know something is wrong with your life, but you cannot understand what it is. You remember how good your life used to be and how much fun it was, but you cannot work out what has gone wrong, for you are in the Darkness - and in the Darkness you cannot see.

You are alone. Your friends drifted away from you because in their eyes you had been behaving strangely and they were frightened by your behaviour. You had changed into someone they didn't recognise and so, fearful about why you had changed and not understanding the reason, they left you.

It was not their fault, neither was it yours.

Now you find you cannot cope with the things that you used to. You know you should be able to and yet your mind simply cannot handle the things it handled before.

You feel it must be able to, but yet it cannot.

You have become the super-reactionary to everything and everyone around you. Small, everyday problems become huge, insurmountable obstacles. Things said to you in jest you take to heart with the utmost seriousness and they strike deep into you, wounding your already broken Spirit.

You find yourself always sleeping, unable to rise even during daylight.

You find yourself unable to sleep and you become a zombie.

You have the greatest difficulty reading, watching television or listening to the radio.

You cannot eat and your weight tumbles.

You eat all the time and your weight explodes.

Either way you hate yourself.

You are like a rudderless, empty vessel tossed by violent, stormy seas on a dark, forbidding night.

Your mind clings desperately to something or someone because, as it recognises its inability to process thoughts normally, it fears it is dying.

That thing or person that it clings to becomes your mind's priority and you think about them one hundred percent of the time. You are unable to think about anything else. You are clinging on to the thought of them for dear life and yet you do not realise what is happening.

Deep, deep down inside you there is a pervading Fear of the Unknown about this dreadful change in your life and it is the Stress of this great Fear that drives the Darkness onward, keeping you in its downward spiral, perpetuating your wretched existence.

You are crying out in the Darkness without realising it, because you have no conception of where you are.

You are tumbling and stumbling blindly along in the all-consuming, life-threatening void of the Darkness of Depression.

I am a Sacred Spirit

I am a Child of God

I am a LifeTraveller

And

We're All In This Together

71

Chapter 9.

WHAT ON EARTH HAPPENED?

I know these things about the Darkness because I have travelled there.

I have plumbed the depths of Depression and drifted in the Void of Hopelessness as my consciousness has finally given in to the beating by The System and I have to tell you something about my experience that you will really be able to identify with:

I didn't like it one little bit.

One of the most important and yet unlikely things to understand about STLD is that it is an absolutely perfectly normal state for a Sacred Spirit to find themselves in.

How can this possibly be?

Well, believe it or not, you are not alone when you are in the Darkness. Millions upon millions of Living Consciousnesses are constantly caving in to the battering by The System. Millions upon millions of Sacred Spirits suddenly find themselves in the Darkness and you and I have been travelling the journey that has shown us how it can be a perfectly natural place for a Living Consciousness to be driven to.

What has happened is that You, the Living Consciousness, have been battered by The System all your life with traumas, anxieties, disappointments and fears. The Noise of Life and The Artillery Bombardment have finally managed to beat your living consciousness into submission. Now your very Core Being is exhausted and drained and lies shattered on the Rocks of Life.

In desperation it clings to thoughts or people, but people don't cling to you for very long. It knows that something is desperately wrong, but it doesn't understand what it is. It knows that it is no longer functioning as it should as it spirals ever downward, reacting to everything that happens both inside itself and out there in life.

During this period of having lost your Core Being, with your mind rebounding and ricocheting off every thought it encounters in its desperation to function properly, you may well start asking yourself those most dreadful and ultimate of questions.

Is this all there is?

Is this all my life is about?

Is this all my life is going to be?

Do I really want to remain a part of this nightmare?

You are consumed by the greatest of Fears, deep down inside, and that Fear is Stress and that Stress holds you in the downward spiral.

It is the Fear of the Unknown, the worst fear of all, of not knowing where you are, where your life has gone and why any of this has happened to you.

Chapter 10.

DISTANT GLIMMER.

But now two weapons have arrived into the beginnings of what will become your armoury in the fight to regain your life. One is your knowledge that fear is only set up by you and no one and nothing else and the other is your awareness of where you are and how you got there - and that where you are is a perfectly normal place to find yourself.

So just say to yourself, 'Oh well, I'm in the Darkness. I'm in Depression that's all and it's a perfectly normal and understandable place for me to be. After all, Jess said so.'

This new awareness about your situation means that you have already won your first battle, believe me, because it hugely reduces the Fear of the Unknown and begins to let you realise that there is nothing at all in this world to fear but fear itself.

Remember? That old impostor that you did such a good job of setting up all on your own?

Did God teach us Fear, or did we teach it to ourselves?

So, with the realisation of this, it is now time to let go of your Fear and make yourself at home in the Darkness. Yes, I'm serious, just make yourself at home in the Darkness, where there is nothing at all to fear, before we set out on our road back to the Light.

Together.

If you are way down there in the Depths of the Darkness it may not feel as though there is any great change in you at this time because these thoughts of awareness will be happening within your mind at the very same level that your base Fear likes to operate at. But this increasing awareness of your predicament will already be counteracting that Fear and registering even a few such thoughts will be a beginning.

This awareness that you now have about your situation will begin to empower you, although it may not feel like it at first. No longer do you have to wonder about what has gone wrong, or where you are, or how you got there, or whether you are somehow 'different' from everyone else.

Now you begin to understand why your friends drifted away. You have not been yourself, the person they originally knew, you have become someone else who, to them, acted strangely, someone they did not recognise. It has been they who have been suffering from the Fear of the Unknown - about you. They didn't know why you changed and found it abnormal against everything The System had always taught them about people and consequently it frightened them. As I said, it was not their fault, neither was it yours, so let's you and I go forwards together and a little later I will show you how you can bring them back into your life.

I am a Sacred Spirit

I am a Child of God

I am a LifeTraveller

And

We're All In This Together

Chapter 11.

THE GREATEST HEALER.

Now is the time for me to introduce you to the greatest healer of STLD on planet Earth. Now is the time for you to meet a healing force so powerful that it can bring Light to your Darkness and eventually banish it from whence it came.

The greatest healer of Stress, Tension, Loneliness and Depression on the face of the Earth, my friend, is You.

No, don't throw the book in the trash. I know you maybe don't believe me, but you are going to, that I promise. I'm not saying that you don't need the services of a good doctor or a trained therapist. But You are the greatest healer of yourself in terms of STLD because there is simply so much that you can do to help to heal yourself and I'm going to prove it to you now, as we set out together on our journey back from the Darkness.

How can you possibly begin to heal yourself when we both know where you are and the dreadful state you are in?

First of all by your awareness of where you are and how you got there and your consequent eradication of that deep seated Fear of the Unknown. Secondly, by becoming aware of the predicament you find yourself in, you must realise that you quite simply cannot handle what you handled before in your life and that You, the Living Consciousness, cannot cope with the things that you used to.

Then you need to realise that you are still being constantly bombarded by the System, day in and day out, and that is what brought you to this dreadful place and that is what is keeping you in the downward spiral. It is everything that has been occurring right up to now in your life that has brought you to this point.

You are going to have to change some things if you want out of the spiral and you are going to have to embrace that change wholeheartedly if you want to get back to the Light.

If you want your life back.

Chapter 12.

THE NEIL ARMSTRONGS.

So what can you do?

To start healing yourself all you need to begin doing are what I call 'The Neil Armstrongs'.

You need to take one small step for You, one small step that will become one giant leap away from STLD.

It will need to be something really simple, something as simple and mundane as making yourself a cup of tea. So let us use this just as an example. But this time you are going to make your cup of tea very differently.

Do you know that this is how some people actually make a cup of tea?

They rush into the kitchen, grab the kettle, blast the water into it, slam it down and turn it on. They grab a teabag, throw it into a mug, go to get a spoon, answer the phone and start writing things to do in their diary at the same time. The kettle boils, they grab it, slosh the water into the mug, swirl the teabag around and drop it into the trash, splashing milk and showering sugar into the mug as fast as they can go. Then they burn their mouths because the tea is too hot, so they pour half of it away and fill it up with cold water so that they can bolt it down, grab their things, rush out of the door and hit the street running!

This is **exactly** what has got to stop!!

This is a really good example of the kind of thing that has most likely been wrong in your life for far too long, although it is just a tiny example of a multitude of things that you do and how you do them.

This kind of rushing through your life absolutely must stop.

I cannot emphasise this enough. Anyway it is anathema to an Englishman like me to see tea prepared in such a way!

It is supposed to be a relaxing drink!

Remember?

THE CUP OF TEA

When you are in the Darkness you must learn to do things in a calm and measured fashion. You must stop the rush that is forcing your mind to process too many thoughts and that produces a total lack of appreciation within you for all the things that you are doing.

From now on you are going to say to yourself,

"I am going to make a special cup of tea specifically for me. This is my cup of tea and I am going to take the time and trouble to make it just the way I like it and I am going to savour every last drop of it."

Boy, is that different to what you used to do!

So you take the kettle and calmly pour in your water, make sure it is plugged in correctly and switch it on. It is your friend, after all it heats the water for you. Then you select your favourite tea bag, the one you really want to make your cup of tea with, English Breakfast, Earl Grey, Camomile, Herb, whatever you really, really feel like. But this time you think about that land far away across the world where this tea was grown, especially for you. You think about how it must have been harvested and transported to you in cargo ships and trucks, after which some kind person took the care to conveniently package it for you. You get your favourite cup or mug and you say to yourself or, even better, you say out loud,

"I am going to make this cup of tea for me, with my favourite tea. I am going to have it in my favourite mug and I am determined that I am really going to enjoy it."

You select your milk and sugar, if that is what you take in your tea, and the kettle boils. Without rushing at any stage you pour in the water and make sure your cup of tea is absolutely perfect, just the way you like it. Then you take it and go and sit in your favourite chair and relax as you savour every last drop and feel the good that it is doing you. And, most importantly of all, you register deep within you that you are doing all of this for You - to make yourself feel better.

If you are someone who has never suffered STLD then this may well sound like utter nonsense. Perhaps you think a person just needs to be told to 'pull themselves together'? Well this is one of the most callous, heartless, thoughtless, unfeeling, uncaring, ridiculously nonsensical things you could ever say to a fellow Sacred Spirit who is in the Darkness.

When someone is in the condition I have been describing they may well be having a tough time just making themselves a cup of tea, never mind 'pulling themselves together'. And just how precisely are they supposed to do that?

When people make this dreadful statement to someone it tells a lot about themselves and what it tells leaves a lot to be desired. I am being polite here!

It shows a lack of Love, of understanding, of concern, of a desire to help and it shows an unacceptable state of denial.

So let us examine what has happened to you, especially if you are someone who is in the Darkness, after you have made your cup of tea

You have taken a first very small step for yourself. You have shut all other thoughts out of your consciousness and concentrated on doing You some good. So what have you done in reality by taking this one small and extremely simple step?

You have turned the entire process of STLD and its downward spiral on its head.

You have begun the task of levelling the Slippery Slope.

You have gone from being a frightened, nervous reactionary to being a calm, proactive Being, helping yourself.

You have done something positive for You and, whilst you were concentrating on making Your cup of tea and savouring and appreciating every drop, your consciousness was allowed a critical change, maybe for the first time.

You pushed the Noise of Life and the Artillery Bombardment away for those few minutes that you concentrated on making your cup of tea and the Living Consciousness that you are was able to rest from the onslaught. No longer was it cannoning from thought to thought or petrified by The Fear of the Unknown. It was able to perform a simple task and concentrate on simple thoughts that were proactive for You.

My, my, what a change.

Congratulations.

You have just lit a candle in your Darkness.

And how much Darkness will it take to extinguish your candle?

Chapter 13.

LOOKING AFTER YOU.

You may be a person who, for all of your life, has looked after other people. Well now the time has come for you to look after You. This is not selfish in any respect, this is self-preservation. How selfish it would be of you to continue on your downward spiral, to just keep going possibly right on out of this world and rob those who love you and those you have yet to meet of your presence here and the good you would be able to do them.

To rob them and yourself of your ability to do good here upon the Earth, that is selfish, my friend.

That is really selfish.

If you do not look after yourself you just might not be around to look after other Sacred Spirits anymore.

You need to take the time to heal yourself.

As the bombardment from The System beats you down you slip through all kinds of shades of grey before you fall into the Darkness of Depression. You do not notice these shades of difference in your life and so you are slipping backwards all the time without realising it. When you set out on the road back to the Light you will find that for a long, long time you will be casting off these shades of grey. You will go one, two or three months and suddenly feel better, stronger and realise that you had not been completely recovered before.

These shades of grey colour your life the wrong way whilst you are on the slide and colour your life the right way on your climb back.

Don't kid yourself that none of this is happening to you, that you'll be O.K., that you can take it. We are all human.

Taking time to heal yourself at any stage of slipping down through these shades of grey will reverse the process and you owe it to yourself and those around you to make the effort to heal yourself from any possible slide into STLD.

NEIL ARMSTRONG 2

THOUGHTLESSNESS.

It is important for you to realise that you cannot do what you did before. You may be able to do those things again one day, but right now your fractured consciousness cannot take more than one small step at a time.

So here is another one:

You do whatever it takes to find somewhere quiet to sit and relax undisturbed and then you close your eyes and try to banish all thought, so that you can just drift in a panacea without a single, solitary thought entering your mind.

This is hard to do when you are in the Darkness with your mind careering around as a response to not being able to function properly and at first you might find this exercise nigh on impossible. When I first tried to do this I was in the Darkness and it was not three seconds before a thought entered my mind. Today I can hold that drifting, thoughtless state for about as long as I want, which is interesting considering that for years my teachers wrote on my school reports that this was precisely what I was brilliant at doing in class.

But if you are able to manage just a few seconds and then practice at extending that amount of time, you will find your consciousness thanks you for it. It thanks you for not having to work at all, not having to process all those continuous thoughts for the first time in......... years?

And you will feel the difference. Go ahead and try it.

You are doing something that enables your consciousness to rest and believe me when I tell you that it needs to be rested more and more. The more you practice shutting out all thought and just BEING, the more your consciousness can begin to heal. Do this exercise often and don't stop doing it. I still do it today and at the time of writing this I am two years from when I first tried it.

It is important to realise that I am not talking about the kind of rest your consciousness gets when you are asleep, for I believe that this is a different kind of rest. The rest I am talking about is specifically for your consciousness whilst you are awake. I know a lady who could barely get out of bed for three years during Depression and I wonder whether that long sleep was beneficial to her or whether repeating this exercise of thoughtlessness whilst she was awake might not have helped quicken her recovery.

Whenever you are Stressed or Depressed try to clear your mind and think of nothing. Your consciousness will thank you for it.

You have lit another candle in your Darkness.

Chapter 14.

THE LONG AND WINDING ROAD.

No one can simply throw a switch and heal themselves from the ravages of STLD. It has been a Long and Winding road you have travelled down into the Darkness and it will be a Long and Winding Road you will have to travel to get back to the Light. But it is a much more pleasurable road, because once you start doing things for yourself, healing yourself little by little and feeling the effect of this healing, you will eagerly become the source of your own empowerment.

You now know that it was everything that you have done in your life up to the point of your freefall into the Darkness that got you there. The road you travelled brought you to this point, so from this point on you must change your road. You must analyse and stop doing all the things you were doing in your life that drove you to this despair and you must be utterly ruthless about cutting them out of your existence.

Can't do it?

Your life too complicated?

Constrained by one thing or another?

Uh-Oh! There's The System talking, the very same System that got you to where you are now. Change your life. Cut out the Stressful things. Be determined to change your whole life if you have to, in the realisation that if you don't look after yourself................

When you realise that you can only take small steps on the road to recovery and that you can only cope with a couple of things, instead of the 5,000 a day that you used to (especially if you are a housewife with kids), it will surely make sense to you that you need to change what has gone before.

So don't just sit there and agree with me... DO IT!

NEIL ARMSTRONG 3.

HOWLING AT THE MOON.

When I was at my worst, having lost 34lbs. in 12 weeks and having spent most of that period vomiting and unable to sleep, the woman who my shattered consciousness was clinging to for life support gave me a brutal elbowing out of the way and went back to her previous boyfriend, her plan all along I believe. And when I was telling my doctor about this as he whacked another massive dose of Vitamin B Complex into my backside he said to me,

"No wonder I can't cure you, you're in Depression."

"No, I'm not."

"Yes, you are."

"No, I'm not."

He looked at me, and to give him his due he had not known me before the STLD had hit me, and he said,

"You haven't got a clue what I'm talking about, have you?"

"No. Sorry, but I've never been depressed in my life."

"Well, I'm telling you that is what is wrong with you and that we are going to have to make a start from this point."

He first of all got rid of my underlying Fear of the Unknown by explaining to me a thing or two about Depression. Then he told me that I needed to let it all out, get it out of my system, that all my fear, anxiety, hurt, loneliness, stress and trauma were tearing me apart and that I just had to let them out.

He wanted me to go and Howl at the Moon!

So I went to friends a couple of hours drive from where I was at the time in South Africa. They weren't really close friends, but when they saw me they were horrified. I was just a skeleton and they told me later that they had thought I had only a few days left to live.

They drove me to a remote beach where they were going to do some beach casting. When we got there they looked at me, pointed down the several miles of empty sand and said,

"Some of us have been where you are now with this woman having done this to you. Go, walk the beach and do what you want. We'll be here all day."

And so I left them and walked the beach. I hadn't got a mile before a rage of shouting and screaming came upon me. I ranted and raved, picked up stones and pieces of flotsam and hurled them as far as I could. I was a man possessed.

I fired question after question at God:

Why do I have this pain?

Why have you done this to me?

What have I ever done wrong?

I've never hurt another human being!

You know I am a good person, so why do I have so much pain?

After half an hour of yelling and throwing I could yell and throw no more. In my weakened state I had become exhausted and could only stand there on the miles of golden sand with just the sun, the surf and the wind and there was my answer, although I did not realise it at the time.

Out over the sea the blue sky had a steely, somehow impenetrable, all-powerful presence about it as if there was an enormous force out there, something listening, watching, waiting for me to vent the churning, pent up feelings inside. There was no answer from some booming voice, no dramatic happening and thankfully no gigantic letters in the sky spelling out 'The End' across the heavens; but there was definitely something out there and so I stood, exhausted and in awe of this sheer presence that seemed to be looking at me, waiting.

Perhaps you need to go and Howl at the Moon. Not so easy if you live in the city, but if you can go out into nature and just let go, let all those pent up feelings come pouring out of you, you will find your answer is out there, looking at you, understanding where you are in your life, waiting to help you heal.

To vent these things you have held inside, where they turn like a knife in your guts, keeping you under Stress, will bring you such relief and as soon as you start to vent your feelings you will begin to feel better and really know that you are on the road back to the Light.

You will have lit another candle in your Darkness.

I am a Sacred Spirit

I am a Child of God

I am a LifeTraveller

And

We're All In This Together

NEIL ARMSTONG 4.

THE CRYING GAME.

Do you find you easily burst into tears? Good for you. It's one of the best releases there is and the more you do it the better. I once met a lady whose therapist had told her never to cry, that she must stop it immediately she felt it coming on and keep those emotions inside her and not let them out.

This is not only absolute rubbish, but to my mind it is patently dangerous!

Never lock those traumatic feelings of STLD inside you where they can twist and turn and eat away at you and constantly do you damage.

If God gave you the ability to cry, why do you think he did that? In order for you to deny the emotions that lead to you crying? No. Crying is an integral part of giving an outlet to those feelings you can no longer contain, nor are you supposed to.

The reason why you suddenly burst into tears is because you have all those traumas, fears, anxieties and bottled up emotions inside you and they simply come welling up over the top. You're too full of them and you need to let them out and you must let them out.

You go right ahead and have a jolly good cry and we both know you'll feel better afterwards.

There is absolutely nothing wrong with crying.

You're just letting it all out, that's all.

And whilst we're on about crying, what about laughing? Laughter is such a great healer, for while you are laughing all the cares and worries of life fall away and there stands the real You.

If you can listen to something or see something or be with someone who makes you laugh then that is what you should be doing, getting a cardio-vascular workout from laughing, which in turn will dissipate your Stress.

You will have lit another candle in your Darkness.

TALKING TO GOD.

Do you ever talk to God?

I went back to my old school in the UK recently – that was a mistake as they grabbed me and put me in charge of raising money for the school whilst I was in South Africa. On the very day I was about to send out my begging letter I received an email from an old school chum who was in South Africa and whom I had been at school with all those years ago.

We met up and it turned out that his girlfriend was having spiritual experiences, generating a great fear in her – a Fear of the Unknown. She didn't understand what was happening. She had begun to be able to tell what John, my old school chum, was thinking, so much so that it had unnerved him too. The previous night he had got out of bed, saying that he had to go and do something, and she had said,
"I know, you're going to go and send a fax to your father."
John nearly dropped on the floor because the thought of doing this had only just entered his mind!
Whilst we talked I began to understand that John held no truck with the spiritual side of life and at one point I asked him,
"Do you ever talk to God?"

"Oh, no." he replied.

"Well, what do you do when things get tough for you?"

"I go for a long walk in the woods and talk it all out with myself."

"And does that work for you?"

"Yes it does."

I thought about this for a moment and then I asked,

"When you go for these long walks and talk things out, are you talking to yourself 100% of the time?" He thought for a while and then he said,

"50% of the time."

He had realised that the other 50% of the time he had really been talking to God.

The System of Life can so easily divorce us from our being able to talk to God.

Do you ever rant and rave at God? I've met so many people who do. They blame God for everything that has gone wrong or is going wrong in their lives. They curse and yell and swear at God for failures in their relationships, losing their jobs or their inability to 'succeed'.

On the one hand they are doing a good thing, they are giving vent to their feelings and letting them out, a great therapy, as we have discussed. But on the other hand they are denying God and themselves the opportunity to access each other. After all if you were to curse and swear at me I would not be able to access you, nor you me until you stopped doing it.

If you are one of these people, have you ever had an answer from God when you have ranted and raved at him? If you have you have been extremely lucky, for I believe that God cannot access you and you cannot access God until you stop your ranting. In the meantime he is watching and listening and waiting for you to get it all out of your system, just like he was with me that day on the beach.

God never answers you? Hardly surprising if you're hurling all those insults at him, is it? Anyway, what did you expect would happen if God did answer you? A massive peal of thunder, a flash of lightning, an explosion of fire and brimstone and out of the smoke would step an elderly man with white hair and a flowing white beard, dressed in white robes and leaning on a staff, whilst Cherubim and Seraphim winged their way around him and a choir of heavenly Angels sang in the background and he would point at you and say,
"You! I command you to…………."

I'm sorry to disappoint you, really I am, but I don't think that God works quite in this way, although if this does happen to you I will be extremely jealous! (Wait a minute, no I won't, that would be **me** setting up a non-existent Jealousy Centre that would drain **my** energies!).

You see, I believe that God stands at the shoulder of every Sacred Spirit, ready to help as soon as he is accessed.

He is around you all the time and he never, ever goes away, not even in your darkest moments or, perhaps, especially not in your darkest moments.

That is why you are never, ever alone.

Especially when you are on your own.

So how do you access God?

First by pushing away the Noise of Life and the Artillery Bombardment that the System is hurling at you – and making some time for You.

Second by letting all of your lifetime's indoctrination under The System fall away. Everything the System has taught you and all your preconceived ideas, notions, reactions and fears have to be laid aside. A hard thing to do, but give it your best shot and win yourself some respite from it all.

Third by standing in front of God in a state of total honesty and opening yourself to him. You do this by holding an honest conversation with him and believe me when I say that real honesty is the key, for without it don't even bother trying. You might tell him that you feel you have wasted some of your life, which I can assure you that you have not, it has all been part of your learning experience.

You might tell him that you know he is there to guide you and that you have now reached the point where you are ready to do his bidding if he will show you the path you should take.

This is just one example of how to talk to God, but there are many others and I am sure you will think of your own way of talking to him. After my experience on the beach I began talking to God a lot and I noticed that I was talking to him in a completely different manner than I had done as a child, when I had begged and pleaded with him to stop 'nasty' things happening to me and that my life was terrible and that my world was ending and that he must change it all.

One memorable conversation I had not so long ago went like this,
"I know I have not been doing very well, but we both know you made me with an inferior brain and so I am a little slow on the uptake. I know you are sending signs to guide me, but they have become an avalanche and I'm just not that good at sorting them out. So please, Lord, make the signs less, but make them great, big obvious ones, so that I can understand them and then I'll be able to use them to guide me."

I have shortened the conversation, but you get the gist of it. Shortly afterwards massive signs came to me, people entered my life and suddenly I had started a website and printed my first book, without having intended to do so and then I found that I also knew that the book you are reading now, my second book, was the one that God really wanted me to write. A book that would be of help to another Sacred Spirit.

So what are these signs, signals or nudges that God sends to each of us?

Everything that happens to you, everything that comes your way, everything you see and hear, in fact absolutely everything that goes on in your life. Once you access God and stand before him in open honesty (liars and cheats get nowhere as the Lord knows our thoughts) and ask him to show you the path he has intended for you, the signs will come. But you have to be constantly aware and looking for them and your mind has to be open to receiving them.

Many of the signs come as coincidences, which in reality are occurrences that are meant to be. Others come via the people you meet, something that happens that resonates with you, something you hear on the radio or see on the television, that spectacular view, that cold wind, that bird, that tree, that colour, that light, that special place and many more.

But how do you read them?

You simply recognise one of these things as being a sign, concentrate on it and try to get the meaning from it and then pass it by, don't dwell on any one thing too long and gradually the messages, the signs and the nudges will lead you on to your path. And keep talking to God as often as you can about the signs and what meaning might be in them for you.

You realise that this book, the fact that you bought it and that you are reading it is a message, a sign, a nudge, don't you?

So when you make the time to talk to God in open honesty remember that he is always listening and that he stands ready to help if you will only access him, that he does work in mysterious ways, but that if you open your eyes you will see him at work in your life and you might just be amazed at what happens to you over the coming months.

Do not expect a miracle and do not expect things to happen at once, just look for the gradual changes in your life that will come, recognise and grasp opportunities with both hands as soon as they appear and follow the path that he unfolds before you.

You may have some problems. You may not be able to achieve total honesty with yourself and with God. You might cheat by saying that God told you to do certain things as an excuse for doing them, or God told you not to do certain things, or use God as a cover for misbehaviour. Who are you fooling? Only yourself. You cannot fool God for he sees and knows everything that you do, think and feel.

You will just be living a lie.

If you don't operate with a huge dollop of honesty you won't be accessing God at all.

I talked with yet another lady some time ago (I do talk with men as well!), she was the ex-wife of someone I had met and he was concerned about her. We sat and talked for three hours. I had immediately seen that she had problems from the state of her house and guessed she had a drink problem on top of everything else. She told me her life had been one constant stream of visits to therapists. She now had no money and had hit rock bottom.

The following evening she called me and told me that all I had done was leave her with a lot of unanswered questions, to which I replied,

"If you are telling me that after years of treatment from all kinds of therapists you still do not have the answers to any of the questions I put in your mind yesterday, then you are living in denial of yourself, you are hiding in your visits to therapists. The answer to every question you have just asked me lies within you, God put the answers there when he made you.

It is time to look for the answers within yourself and remember that God is standing at your shoulder, always ready to help whenever you choose to access him."

She didn't call me again, but a few months later her ex-husband told me that she had stopped drinking, had got herself a job and was determined to make something of her life again. She had looked inside herself and found the answers that would carry her forward.

The Lord truly does work in mysterious ways.

Talking with God will light another candle in your Darkness

NEIL ARMSTRONG 6.

COUNTING COLOURS.

From the age of eight I was lucky enough to be taken on holiday fishing for Atlantic Salmon in Scotland and we used to go to an old country house hotel that for me was Valhalla. Those fishing holidays were more than special because not only was I fishing for what to me was the King of Fish, but I would also meet up with one of the most incredible Sacred Spirits it has been my privilege to come across.

His name was Jimmy MacLean (pronounce MacLane) and he was the ghillie (the gamekeeper on the river) at the hotel, where he had saved my life in the river when I was 10 years old. On one particular day, when I was thirteen, he took me fishing during a summer heat wave.

The river was low, showing us her bare bones and no Salmon were running, but we went fishing anyway as there was just a chance that we might catch a Trout. My shirt burnt my back and it wasn't long before the heat brought on my boredom and I gazed over the side of the boat as we sat at anchor in the sluggish current. After a while Jimmy said to me,

"How many colours can you see?" I looked at him, surprised at this question and not understanding it.

"Down there, on the riverbed, how many colours can you see?"

I looked over the side and counted eight colours on the rocky riverbed, some four or five feet below me. Jimmy shook his head,

"Oh, I think there are more than that. Try again."

I did so and this time I counted twelve colours. He shook his head and came to join me and there we were, this giant of a man and a small boy peering into the river whilst leaning over the side of the boat, which was tilted at a precarious angle, and Jimmy MacLean taught me how to count colours.

He showed me all the different shadings and how the shadings changed the colours and how to look at them through the eye of the artist. Together we identified all kinds of colours – Magenta, Ochre, Indigo, Maroon, Violet, Vermilion, Crimson, Turquoise, Slate Blue, Slate Grey, Olive, Khaki, Purple, all were there on the rocky riverbed below.

When we had counted colours into the high thirties we stopped and sat back in the boat.

"Always remember a saying that we have in Scotland," Jimmy said to me, "There are those who look and there are those who see."

A truer saying is hard to find and there have been many times in my life in all kinds of situations when I have kicked myself for looking, but not seeing.

So maybe when you do Neil Armstrong 1 and you make yourself that cup of tea and you go and sit in your favourite chair and look out of your window at your favourite view, or you look at a plant, or a painting or a photograph, or the pattern of your carpet, you might start counting colours. Slowly, methodically, without rush or pressure and whilst you are counting them remember that great maxim:

'There are those who look and there are those who see.'

You know what you are doing by now, don't you?

Pushing away The System, The Noise and the Artillery Bombardment and letting your consciousness rest from their assault.

Letting your Consciousness Rest and Heal.

You have lit another candle in your Darkness.

NEIL ARMSTRONG 7.

THE CHILD INSIDE.

When I was at my worst point of Depression I went to see a therapist friend on a professional basis and she was horrified to see the state I was in. She asked if I had a picture of myself as a child. I didn't but she said I must get hold of one and keep it with me at all times and look at it constantly.

"You have to understand that it is the 'child inside' of you that is hurting, that is screaming and crying out with pain in the Darkness. And what do you do when you see a child hurting so bad that its pain comes out in screams? You take it by the hand, take care to heal its pain and lead it away from the darkness. All your life you have looked after others, now it is time for you to look after the child inside of you."

I thought about what she had said a great deal and it resonated deeply within me and so I began taking care of the 'child inside'.

Some time later I was helping a lady who was deep in Depression and she said that she didn't really understand how to help the child inside. I told her that all she had to do was to start asking the child within herself questions like these:

"What do you feel like doing now?"
'I feel like having a cup of tea and counting colours'.
"Then that is what we'll do."

"What do you feel like doing now?"
'I feel like having an nice hot bath'.
"Then that is what we'll do."

"What do you feel like doing now?"
'I feel like going for a long, quiet walk on the beach'.
"Then that is what we'll do."

"What do you feel like doing now?"
'I just want to sit here and watch the waves and relax and think'.
"Then that is what we'll do."

"What do you feel like doing now?"
'I feel like seeing my old friend who I haven't seen for so long."
"Then that is what we'll do."

And so on. You are taking the 'child inside' you by the hand and giving it the comfort and care that it needs and all the time you are healing that child, you are healing yourself.

You have lit another candle in your Darkness.

NEIL ARMSTRONG 8.

LET EVERYONE KNOW.

Have your friends drifted away from you, increasing your feeling of loneliness? This, as I said earlier, is because they no longer recognise you as the person they first befriended and they Fear the Unknown that is around you. It is not their fault or yours, it is just a natural phenomenon to do with your suffering.

What you should do, now that you know what is wrong with you and why it has occurred, is go out to absolutely everyone you know and tell them about it. Letters, emails, phone calls, however you do it go out to everyone, family, friends and every acquaintance you can ever remember meeting. What you must do is make them aware of your condition and so erase their underlying Fear of the Unknown about you.

Tell your family and friends something like this:

"I'm terribly sorry that I have not been myself lately and that consequently our friendship has waned, but I have found out that I am suffering from clinical depression and that is what has changed me and that is why I have been struggling just to make it through each day. I would really appreciate it if we could continue our friendship, which I have always valued highly. I need as much help as possible if I am going to get through this."

Say something like this to your acquaintances:

"I know we do not know each other well, but I have been told that I am suffering from clinical depression and I'm having trouble just making it through each day. Do you know anyone who has been through this who I could talk to or have you any experience at all of depression? I would really appreciate any help you might be able to give me."

My friend, stand back and prepare to be amazed.

The above is something along the lines of what I did when I discovered what was wrong with me and the reaction was nothing short of miraculous.

You see, I've already told you that when we are born we are each made as a 100% Loving Being and once people know and understand what is wrong with you, and thus their Fear of the Unknown begins to evaporate, they will all want to help and the Sacred Spirit's tendency towards the Power of Love will come shining through.

I received an overwhelming wave of love and help from all over the world after I went out to everyone and told them what was wrong with me. Even people who didn't know me were getting in touch via friends and offering their advice. It is quite simply the biggest boost that you can ever get and you begin to realise that you are not alone and so that insidious feeling will ebb away.

Love and moral backup is out there for you, just go and tap into it.

You will have lit another candle in your Darkness.

NEIL ARMSTRONG 9.

YOUR SANCTUARY.

O.K. For this one you need to close your eyes, calm yourself down and take yourself off to a sanctuary. This will be a place that you can take yourself to whenever you feel STLD tugging at you.

This should be a special place, perhaps a place that you were once incredibly happy in. It can be indoors or outdoors, it doesn't matter as long as it is a place you identify with strongly that gives you security and peace of mind. If you can't think of a place like that, then you can construct a special one all of your own which will be as good as your imagination can make it.

What you have to do is envisage the place precisely and take yourself there in your mind. When you get there you want to be able to clearly see everything, all the colours and everything that you love about it.

You should be able to hear the sounds you associate with it, the birds or maybe the music. You should be able to feel it, the wind, the warmth of the sun or the rain on your face. You should be able to smell it, the flowers or the cooking. You should be able to taste it, the wine or the food. You should be totally immersed there in your mind, wrapped up in the safety and security of your sanctuary.

See it, feel it, touch it, smell it, taste it, know it.

You may need to work at this to be able to get a hold of it, but it's a great therapy.

When things got tough for me I used to go and lie on my bed, close my eyes and take myself off to the Rock Pool, a place on the river where Jimmy and I used to go fishing. Since then I have physically been back to the Rock Pool three times and a powerfully spiritual place, associated with some of the happiest times of my youth, it is.

Funnily enough I was using the services of a genius lady who was teaching me 'whole brain techniques' (could have used those at school) that helped enormously on my way back from the Darkness. She asked me how I saw myself at the Rock Pool. Well, I suppose I saw myself as the rock that shelved down into the water on the other bank, some sixty metres/yards away.

Then she asked me how I saw the woman who had dumped me and where was she at the Rock Pool. I saw her as fire, as flames on the opposite bank to the Rock.

"And fire cannot cross water, can it?" she asked.

Your Sanctuary can be your saviour.

What is it that you are doing for your consciousness whilst you are resting in your Sanctuary?

You have lit another candle in your Darkness.

NEIL ARMSTRONG 10.

THE HUG.

When you give someone a hug do you just hug them for a second or two and then let go? Well don't. The next time you hug someone go up to them and tell them you want a proper hug and you want it to last for a whole minute. They will be astonished and uncomfortable at first, but you insist that you need to do this because it will do you good and, if you hang on to each other for an entire minute, you will find that it has done them good as well.

Have you ever hugged a tree?

Silly idea, isn't it?

Trees are wonderful things. They stand guardian as windbreaks, they give shelter from heat, rain or wind, they beautify the landscape, many of them changing into a multitude of colours with the seasons, they cloak themselves with snow in winter to give us a splendid picture, they keep our atmosphere healthy and they live a lot longer than we do.

Trees are your friends and you should be happy amongst them. Listen to the wind rustling their leaves, see

117

them standing sentinel over nature in all weathers and rejoice in the fact that God gave us trees.

You are DNA and so is the tree, as is everything that grows, it's just in a different form.

Go and give a tree a real long hug and thank it just for being (learning how to be) and tell it you appreciate that it will be here long after you are gone and that you are glad it will be here to be enjoyed by the next generation.

Hugging a tree can make you feel your own value in nature and it can give you a perspective that you may have lost as The System has worked on you.

Go hug a tree and to hell with what people think!

You will have lit another candle in your Darkness.

NEIL ARMSTRONG 11.

NATURAL HEALING.

STLD ravages your body. It consumes energy from you in huge quantities, making you use up vitamins and minerals and lowering your immune system.

What you do not need is an illness like flu coming in at the very nadir of your depression and hitting you ten times harder than it ought to be able to. We know that you have to take care of You and so that means your overall health, which is where Natural Health Products can really help you.

I am not a doctor and I am not decrying modern drugs, nor am I prescribing that you take Natural Products. I am simply going to show you a few of them, pointing out the benefits of adding them to your armoury and giving you the strongest advice to go and talk to the people who run the best Natural Health Stores you can find, two or three of them if possible (stores, not people!).

It is important to know that Natural, Herbal Products take longer to have an effect than conventional drugs, but that effect can be extremely beneficial. They are not like anti-biotics whereby they go straight into your bloodstream and nail the heck out of any bug they can find.

Natural Products are absorbed slowly and take time to permeate throughout your system on a deep level. So you should take them for a minimum of three months, if not six, to gain real benefit and enjoy their full effect.

Be proactive in this regard, continue taking them in the knowledge that they are working for your benefit and gradually you will feel that benefit. If you take them for a week and then stop taking them, you may well feel no benefit and will continue downwards in the spiral.

St. John's Wort, also known as **Hypericum**, is taken from the plant Hypericum Perforatum and is a mood elevator. It works on your Seratonin and helps to stop distress messages going to your brain. We might call it Nature's Tranquiliser or the Natural Prozac without the side effects. St.John's Wort worked for me, but evidence is now surfacing that indicates it might not mix with some conventional drugs. So if you are on medication you must of course check this out thoroughly.

Echinacea is an immune system stimulant. It will boost your immune system and is effective at the onset of flu, but not as a prevention. It is great for a stress-depleted immune system and taken every day will ward off illnesses. You should not use it all the time though, miss out one week in four as otherwise you will unnecessarily be boosting your immune system for all of that period for no reason. You can get it in a tincture (liquid) or in a capsule, but check them out because sometimes the capsule can be up to ten times stronger.

Propolis. You know when trees are damaged and they ooze that sticky stuff? Well that 'stuff' is a protective agent that stops a virus getting into the tree and killing it. Bees take this stuff and spread it at the entrance to their hives for the same reason. A virus getting into the close community of a beehive would kill the entire community.

Pro – Before.   Polis – The City   (Like Metropolis).

You can get it in Syrup form or Capsule or Throat Spray or Lozenge and you can get it mixed with other things, like Echinacea. Propolis stops bugs from multiplying, so it can help to stop the Common Cold from getting worse and flu from getting a real hold if taken at the onset. You can take it all the time while flu is around. It is good for Sore Throat, Glands and Sinus and apparently it can cure Shingles when sprayed on, although I have no experience of this.

Vitamin B Complex. Vitamin B is the Stress vitamin and will really help your body against the ravages of STLD. You will find you can get a natural B and C complex together.

Detoxification.

You absolutely must detoxify. There is no option as this is a hugely powerful way to help your body fight STLD. The foods and drinks of today are stuffed full of chemicals, toxins, additives and preservatives that can build up within you if your intake is faster than your body is able to clear them. Your liver is the crucial organ in your body for fighting bacteria and it cannot function properly if it is working flat out dealing with a constant build up of toxins and chemicals.

Detoxifying and cleansing your liver so that it can function as originally intended will be of tremendous benefit to you in the fight against STLD as it will enable you to build up your immune system faster. If you don't do it you will continue to keep physically under par, allowing STLD to flourish through your inability to fight back on a physical level.

So a programme of detoxification is a must.

To be sure about Natural Products and their benefits to you always consult your local Health store, as I have recommended, but I usually check with two or three to confirm what to give myself to aid the process of detoxification. For instance Milk Thistle helps your liver and Dandelion works on your kidneys and gall bladder, helping them to detoxify, however there are a great variety of things that you can take for the same purpose and which health stores will advise on.

Alcohol, Drugs and Tobacco all contain toxins and chemicals that your body could well do without. Cut them right out of your life – just do it. Do you want to get back to an enjoyable life again, or not? If you cut them out then keep thinking about the massive fall in your intake of all these things that were doing you no good at all. What a huge advance in your fight against STLD.

In fact Alcohol, Drugs and Tobacco are the very embodiment of The System, holding your life in their grasp so that it is no longer within your own. If you have found you have turned to any or all of them as a comfort from the effects of STLD, then realise that you are hiding inside of the very thing that has been beating you down.

Watch out because their effect upon you in your weakened state, especially that of Alcohol or Drugs, will be far more powerful than normal. They may kid you that you feel a little better for indulging in them, but it will only be a short-term fix and you will be continuing on ever downwards in the spiral. So get out from under their hold with the one determined thought in your mind that you want to get well again and return to an enjoyable life. Believe me when I tell you that you can do it and not only that, but guess who is standing at your shoulder, always ready to help?

Start concentrating on feeding your body only the good stuff. Salads, Vegetables, Herbs, Fruits, Fish, Chicken, but stay off a heavy intake of red meat for a while. If you can buy organically grown produce whilst you are detoxifying, so much the better. Control the portions of what you eat, because even eating the right things will still keep your weight up if you eat tons of them, but lesser portions over a period will help rid you of that bloated feeling.

Cut out Coffee and anything else with caffeine in it, like some Teas. A Homeopath will tell you that Coffee and Mint are two of the most powerful things that you can put in the body, which is why they can nullify some homeopathic remedies. Mint is harmless, but Coffee of course contains Caffeine, which is addictive.

Take Herbal Teas instead, but be prepared for a Caffeine withdrawal headache within 24 to 72 hours of cutting Coffee out. This is perfectly normal as the stored Caffeine comes flooding out of fibre back into your bloodstream. It will only last a couple of days, three at the most. Other toxins will also be flooding into your system for the first week or so and you may not feel too great, but don't worry about it, just drink gallons of water to flush your system through and you will quickly clear them - have faith in the fact that you are on the road to recovery.

The Cleanser.

There is a simple, but highly effective drink that can be of major assistance in cleansing your system.

Buy some fresh herbs and some lemon. Put a selection of these different fresh herbs, such as Rosemary, Basil, Oregano, Parsley and Celery, in a mug with two or three slices of lemon and add boiling water. Sip the resulting brew and you will be taking in the goodness from the herbs and the essential oils from the lemon. It might taste really weird to you at first so you can experiment with various herbs, until you find something palatable. You can even eat the herbs (now cooked!) when you've finished the drink. They certainly won't do you any harm. This intake of a herbal/lemon infusion instead of what you used to drink (think about it) will be of major assistance in your detoxification and you can drink it as often as you like.

Take good care of the body God gave You.

You will have lit another candle in your Darkness.

NEIL ARMSTRONG 12

FOUR LITTLE WORDS

The last of the twelve Neil Armstrongs that I have to give you is by no means the least valuable.

Let us say you are in the Darkness, confused, lonely, depressed or you have just moved to a new town, where you know no one, and you are feeling unnerved deep down and have that creeping Fear of the Unknown, that you are most probably trying to deny.

Or let us say that you have suffered or are suffering terribly. Your life has been destroyed, your world rent asunder, every tenet and belief you held concerning life, people and God has crashed and burned. You can imagine these scenarios for yourself, or maybe you are in one of them right now or you know someone who is.

What would be the most unlikely, most ridiculous, most outrageous, most challenging thing that you could do in any of these situations? It takes some working out, but I stumbled upon it by accident (or was I guided?) and it brought me up short with such a jarring inner shock that suddenly my fears, my problems and my nightmare receded in the light of this development.

It is the most unlikely of things to do when you are demolished in heart and soul, when you are perhaps suffering the grief of bereavement or struggling with some dreadful medical condition. You are in need of help, spiritual, physical, comforting, loving help, the kind that will pick you up, restore you, make you forget, make you better, make you stronger. You are in the depths, your life is a misery, all hope is lost and it feels as if, for you, it is finally all over.

What could you do that would shatter this state, break you out of where you are, catapult your life back upwards towards the Light?

Giving of yourself when you think you have nothing left to give.

Oh, yes it's a tough one. Tough because it seems so ridiculous.

How can you give when you've got nothing left to give?

Because having nothing left is a misconception.

You know when an athlete trains and they push themselves through the pain barrier time and time again? As they do so they find out that even when they think they are exhausted and that their tank is empty there is still something left in there and, once they know this, when they reach the barrier again they have the knowledge that there is more to come, that they can give more.

It is the same with each of us. How many times have we thought we are badly off only to find someone who is much worse off than we are? We think we are at the bottom because of our conception of life, but in reality have we really tested our limits? Even in the Darkness of Depression?

There are four little words you can use to wrench yourself out of your predicament. They are perhaps the last words you would think of uttering:

HOW CAN I HELP?

To be nowhere, to be lost, desolated, broken and deeply troubled and to offer your help to another is the most selfless, most giving, most ultimate of deeds. To go to someone, anyone, whether you know them or not, and simply say to them, 'How can I help?', even if you don't know how you could help if they wanted you to, is to extend the hand of true friendship, to promote the thinking of doing good for others.

To offer help to a fellow Sacred Spirit when in fact it is you who is really in need of help is one of the greatest, most empowering things that you can do.

O.K. So you are going to have to steel yourself in case you get your offer thrown back in your face. Also you are going to have to explain what you are able to do and what you are unable to do, but maybe what you are asked to do will be as simple as washing up some dirty dishes or just sitting with someone who is ill and listening to their story, giving them comfort. Or maybe reading to someone's kids whilst they get a little time to themselves. It doesn't matter what it is or how inconsequential it seems, what matters is that you are giving of yourself selflessly, without looking for a return.

Whilst I was in Depression someone contacted me who was struggling with Depression themselves and I immediately helped them to the best of my ability. In that second I received a jarring shockwave within. I said to God, 'So you see, I have nothing, I am nearly dead myself, but I can still help another – I am learning this lesson you are teaching me'. The lesson turned out to be that God wanted me to help others for the rest of my life – hence the talks I give and hence this book.

But that giving of help swept a feeling of self-empowerment into being and from that moment I followed my new path as someone else contacted me who had problems and that was how my own rehabilitation began on the road back to the Light.

By giving to others.

Try it. Just go to someone, whether you like them or not, whether you think you can help or not, whether you feel your world is over or not and say Four Little Words to them and follow through on their reaction. If they reply that you can help then do so and return to your home in the knowledge that you did something for someone else, when you supposedly had nothing left to give.

After that keep on doing it. Keep going to people and asking them 'How can I help?' and see where it leads you. One thing I can assure you of – your life will change if you keep saying and acting upon these Four Little Words because things will start to happen. The most incredible thing will be that if you can keep doing this you will feel your life has become worthwhile again.

And so it will have.

You will have lit another candle in your Darkness.

Now you have twelve candles burning brightly where there were none before.

Chapter 15.

CHANGING YOUR LIFE.

You remember we were talking about the fact that everything you have been doing in your life up to this time has brought you to this point? Well in the simple Natural Product and Detoxification programme I outlined in Neil Armstrong 11 you will already have begun to change what went before. You may be saying that it is impossible to change your life, but that is just the indoctrination of The System talking for you. If you want to wrest your life back into your own hands from everything that has been dictating to it up until now, you must be bold.

You need to make a list of all the things that you do in a day, in a week, in a month, in a year, in your life. Then get a red pen out and use it as a knife and ruthlessly cut out the major things that adversely affect you, that stress and pressurise you, that dictate to you how your life will be instead of you making that determination. Boldness and ruthlessness with this operation will pay off by handing you your life back.

Remember that you are never alone if this process scares you and I can well understand your trepidation, but a faint heart only comes from the false 'foundations' in your life that The System has laid down as part of its hold upon you.

You are nervous that if these 'foundations' are moved you won't know what to do, or how to be. That is normal. But at least you understand that your life must change or you will remain in the spiral, in the clutches of STLD, dictated to by The System.

How determined are you to take your life back into your own hands?

Your life, no matter how good or bad, is the greatest gift you will ever be given and it belongs to you, to do with as you will, and not to anyone else. If someone else dictates your life to you then you need to examine whether to try to renegotiate your situation with that person or cut them out of your life altogether. Tough talk, I know, but the option for you of staying where and how you are will be much tougher.

Your determination must also centre on changing your life into something you can easily cope with, something that gives you time for You. You may be able to do this by changing jobs, or cutting the three jobs you do back to just one. Examine your financial overheads, maybe sell your house and move to a smaller one, or move further out into the country and so reduce your mortgage/bond payments to something you can easily handle as well as getting closer to nature.

Stop trying to push a humongous great boulder up a humongous great mountain every day of your life and exchange the boulder for a pebble and the mountain for a hill.

Explain to your loved ones what is wrong with you and that you can no longer cope with what you used to. Tell them of your ideas about what you need to do to be able to get well again. If they love you they will agree to make changes, however drastic, to give you the life you need. If they won't agree then you must ask yourself whether they really do love you. This is a question that may strike at the heart of what could have put you in the state you are in today, so don't back away from it, take hold of that situation with both hands and sort it out – now!

It is of paramount importance that you force these life issues through, as they are critical to your recovery and, in the longer term, to your survival.

The System has put the word 'Can't' into your psyche - a word that has been designed to leave you permanently in the spiral.

Take strength from this fact:

Depression is a cleansing of everything bad that has gone before in your life and is a preparation of you for all the good that is to come.

Chapter 16.

FINAL REALISATION.

I could have given you more than twelve Neil Armstrongs, but when I look at these twelve I know that they are more than enough to be of real help to any Sacred Spirit at whatever level of Stress, Tension, Loneliness or Depression might be affecting them. You see you only need to take that first little step and feel its effect and you are hooked, hooked on the road to healing yourself.

Whether you know anything of STLD, or whether you are currently suffering from Stress or you are sliding into, or you are already in the Darkness of Depression there is something of the utmost, crucial importance that you have already done.

When you bought this book you became proactive, wanting to help yourself, wanting to learn what I had to offer (and I sincerely hope I have offered you something worthwhile), wanting to heal either yourself or someone you know.

When you bought this book you already took that first step on your road to recovery, to beating STLD. You changed what had gone before, you began to stop the downwards spiral and, as you read the book and learned of the things within it that can help you, you began your journey on the road back to the Light.

You are on your way.

So now that you have already taken your first step on that road just you make sure that you take other steps that follow on.
Or else!

HEAL YOUR CONSCIOUSNESS.

Take the time to let your consciousness rest and give it the therapies that will allow it to heal and it will bless you, respond and begin to function well again, even though this may take some time.

HEAL YOUR HEART.

Banish Hate, Fear, Anger, Jealousy, Greed and all the emotions of weakness that consume your Life Energy, forever.

Turn to the pure, powerful strength of Love.

Think of yourself being in the Darkness and somehow making an act of selflessness, an act of pure Love to another Sacred Spirit at a time when you think you have nothing to give. That act of selflessness, going to help someone else when you are in trouble yourself, will shine like a beacon in your Darkness, empowering you, restoring your self respect and giving you perspective within your struggle.

Never, ever expect anything in return when you do something for someone out of Love, for that is not pure Love – it is a falseness. Do whatever it is you can and then walk away. Your reward will already be the building of inner strength within you, knowing that you gave and rejoicing in that giving.

Giving money if you are wealthy is not necessarily a dispensation of Love, it is a kindly act, but it does not buy the rewards within that Love produces, nor does it excuse your living a Loveless life towards your fellow Sacred Spirits.

Physically helping someone who may not be your favourite person, whether with sweat and toil or kindly words or plain, patient understanding is the real way forward. I am not decrying the giving of money at all, I am just pointing out that the writing of a check/cheque can produce the thought in you that you have somehow dispensed Love, and in a way you have, but your helping words of wisdom, your personally caring for another soul is the most powerful expression of Loving selflessness that you can make.

Too often we either forget or have never learned this wisdom.

LOOKING AFTER YOU.

Finally, fellow Sacred Spirit, look after the Living Consciousness that you are and the body God gave you and you will be guided on your way back to the Light. It may well turn out to be a Long and Winding Road and one that will test your patience, but as long as your mind and your eyes are open the road will be filled with magical lessons and messages, the Power of Love and the Understanding of God.

Your target is to emerge triumphantly back into the Light and step boldly out into your brand new dawn, into a rising sunlight in your life. You will have worked hard to make yourself whole once more, but through your efforts you will find that you have become a Warmer, more Loving, more Understanding, more Useful, more Resilient and more Enjoyable Sacred Spirit for having suffered the dreadful experience of STLD.

Not only that, but God will be standing right there at your shoulder as ever, ready to help and guide you whenever you access him and ready to watch your progression as you use the signs, the messages and the nudges he will keep sending you to help you along your way.

And that, my friend, is a prize worth fighting for.

Chapter 17.

The Being.

You are simply the most incredible Being, for God has imbued you with countless hidden strengths, qualities and capabilities that you are most likely, as yet, to be unaware of.

You are the supercomputer of all supercomputers.

Your abilities are boundless.

Look at all the senses you have at your command, all the knowledge you have amassed in your life, all the feelings and emotions that forever course through you and all the countless thoughts that you are able to continually process.

When God created you he created the most wondrous Being.

Now you are ready to look fearlessly within yourself – fearlessly because of your overpowering desire to heal yourself and begin living your life in a worthwhile way, to be the most useful that you can be, to make sure that this wondrous achievement of your creation and the life that you have been given will not be wasted, even for one single second.

The Time for You is at Hand

Not tomorrow.

Not next week.

Not next month.

Not next year.

The Time for You is Now.

The answers lie within You.

Start asking yourself the questions.

Good Luck to You, Sacred Spirit.

I am a Sacred Spirit

I am a Child of God

I am a LifeTraveller

And

We're All In This Together

ONE SMALL STEP FOR YOU..........

NEIL ARMSTRONG 1	THE CUP OF TEA
NEIL ARMSTRONG 2	THOUGHTLESSNESS
NEIL ARMSTRONG 3	HOWLING AT THE MOON
NEIL ARMSTRONG 4	THE CRYING GAME
NEIL ARMSTRONG 5	TALKING TO GOD
NEIL ARMSTRONG 6	COUNTING COLOURS
NEIL ARMSTRONG 7	THE CHILD INSIDE
NEIL ARMSTRONG 8	LET EVERYONE KNOW
NEIL ARMSTRONG 9	YOUR SANCTUARY
NEIL ARMSTRONG 10	THE HUG
NEIL ARMSTRONG 11	NATURAL HEALING
NEIL ARMSTRONG 12	FOUR LITTLE WORDS

Lifetravellers.com